The
Wine & Food
of Austria

The
Wine & Food
of Austria

by Giles MacDonogh
Photographs by Manfred Horvath

MITCHELL BEAZLEY

Edited and designed by
Mitchell Beazley Publishers
part of Reed International Books Ltd
Michelin House
81 Fulham Road
London SW3 6RB

A CIP catalogue record for this book is available from the
British Library.

ISBN 0 85533 944 6

Editor: Elizabeth Bellord
Senior Art Editor: Paul Drayson
Production: Sarah Schuman
Executive Editor: Anne Ryland
Executive Art Editor: Tim Foster

Typeset in Imprint by
Servis Filmsetting Ltd, Manchester, England
Origination by Scantrams PTE Ltd, Singapore
Produced by Mandarin Offset
Printed in Hong Kong

Maps by Lorraine Harrison
Index by Hilary Bird

CONTENTS

◆

◆

◆

Du bist wie eine Blume
So hold und schön und rein;
Ich schau' dich an, und Wehmut
Schleicht mir ins Herz hinein.

Mir ist, als ob ich die Hände
Aufs Haupt dir legen sollt',
Betend, daß Gott dich erhalte
So rein und schön und hold.

Heine

FOR IMOGEN AINSWORTH

ACKNOWLEDGEMENTS

This book would not have been possible without the generous assistance of the Österreichische Weinmarketingserviceges in Vienna; and I should like to offer my thanks to Walter Kutscher, Fritz Ascher and Dorli Muhr for all their help. I am grateful also to Karl Mayer who gave me the run of his library in the Weinbauschule in Klosterneuburg and introduced me to the writings of Franz Schams. My thanks too to Geoffrey Kelly in London for liaising with Austria over the book. In Austria itself I had four patient drivers in Martin Kelner, Peter Schleimer, Reinhold Forobosco and Florian Kruse. Martin Kelner deserves a very special word of praise, not only for having driven me about but also for working out my programme of visits and giving me the benefit of his wit and wisdom along the way. He has also read the manuscript and cleared up a number of factual errors.

I should also like to show my gratitude to friends in Vienna who occasionally distracted me from the daily tasting marathons: Adèle Crothers, Professor Dominic and Nora Purcell, Adrian Weissweiler and Christopher Wentworth-Stanley. In London, Jill Cox was kind enough to look over the recipes and make them manageable for the domestic kitchen. My old friend Roderick Blyth has translated the poems in the text, displaying his characteristic ability to see the lighter side of wine.

Giles MacDonogh
London 1992

INTRODUCTION

*A*ustria is in central Europe; at the heart of the old continent. The political geography of the nations around her has changed a good deal this century, and it looks set to change again; but the Austrian core is solid and acts as an anchor in a sea of permanently struggling racial groups.

Austria's Habsburg past made light of race and nationality; pick up the Vienna telephone book and you will be instantly struck by the origins of the names: how few of them are Germanic! All these migrants have made their contribution to Austria's culture: Magyars, Bohemians, Croats, Serbs, Slovenians, Slovaks, Italians, Poles, Turks and Jews. Travel out to the more remote vineyards and pretty soon you will find yourself on a flimsy border erected by the wise old men of 1919. The vines, however, are no respecters of borders: Styria's grape varieties are identical to those of Slovenia (the former Lower Styria); Burgenland's the same as those of Hungary; the Weinviertel's echoed by those in Czecho-Slovakia.

In latitudinal terms, Vienna is on the same line as Paris. The vineyards of the northern Weinviertel are comparable to those of Champagne; those of southern Burgenland to Burgundy. These comparisons of latitude, however, only tell part of the story. Most of France has an Atlantic climate while most of Austria is Continental. The northern Weinviertel is one of the most arid regions in Europe with plenty of sunshine to ripen the grapes. In the south, Styria is wetter; while in the east, Burgenland benefits from the effects of the hot, dry climate of the vast Pannonian plain.

Differences of culture and climate contribute to the variety of Austrian wines: aromatic dry whites and big reds from the Weinviertel in the north; steely, racy whites from the Wachau and Kamptal-Donauland in the centre; wines of great breed from the steep slopes of Vienna and Klosterneuburg; sweet whites and big reds from Burgenland; and the sappy, juicy wines of Styria in the south. Austria really has a wine to match pretty well any taste; which may explain why Austrians are keen on them to the exclusion of virtually anything else.

Sadly, they are not well known abroad. To some degree this is the result of the famous 'wine scandal' of 1985 when a few greedy wine merchants doctored some wine with diethyline glycol to pass off thin musts as a higher *Prädikat* or must weight. The rogues were caught when one of them claimed for the glycol on his income tax return; which must say something about the intelligence of the men involved. There were no more than a couple of dozen criminals involved in the fraud, but the glycol joke has proved a hardy perennial, so that even now when I am preparing for another trip to Austria some wag rings up to say "you won't need a hot-water bottle there!", or something of the sort.

Austrians see it differently: when I was talking to one winemaker in the Thermenregion recently, the scandal reared its head in the usual way. My host, however, was in no way upset about the events of 1985, "*Gott sei Dank!*", he exclaimed "the scandal destroyed those middle-men who were parasites sucking the blood of the growers!" Now this grower and others of his sort does a fine trade selling to customers who seek him out. The Austrian wine trade has virtually disappeared.

The scandal had another positive side: it cut away the dead wood of Austrian wine. Those semi-sweet *lieblich* wines which were made in imitation of German wines in the north were scrapped in favour of dry whites. Flabby sweet wines made by artificially stopping the fermentation gave way to proper dessert wines made from *Botrytis*-affected grapes or by age-old practices leading to the production of *Eiswein* or straw wines; more red wines were made; the old made way for the young and the wines now bear the stamp of youth.

Not surprisingly, it was the Germans who first discovered what was happening in Austria. The Germans and the Austrians speak (something like) the same language, and many Germans are aware that Austria contains a little more than a handful of ski-pistes. Towards the end of the 1980s the news got back to Düsseldorf, Munich and Berlin that the wines of Austria had taken a new direction. The revelation was followed by a stampede for their cars and soon the German wine-drinking public had arrived to buy up for their cellars at home. This book attempts to share the new wines and food of Austria with the rest of the world; while stocks last.

8

◆

CHAPTER I

A History of Austrian Wine

*I*n September 1919 a collection of diplomats and high-ranking military officers gathered together in the small French town of Saint-Germain-en-Laye. Having wound up the German and Ottoman Empires, their job that morning was to reallocate the former possessions of the Habsburg Monarchy. As representatives of one of the losers in the 1914–18 war, the Austrian plenipotentiaries had little choice but to sign away their history with their territories in Hungary, Bohemia, Moravia, Slovenia, Slovakia, Romania, Italy and Poland. Before the ink was dry on the Treaty of Saint-Germain, the delegates had reduced the sprawling bulk of the Austro-Hungarian Empire to a few territories scattered among the eastern outcrops of the Alps, and a handful of more arable provinces situated along the meandering River Danube between Linz and the now Czechoslovakian city of Bratislava.

The present state of Austria is therefore one of Europe's most recent creations; the same age as

The great tun of Klosterneuburg in a 19th-century engraving.

9

Czecho-Slovakia and Yugoslavia. Naturally, though, the history of Austria's German-speaking peoples goes back further than the 70 years of the present state to the tribes who first elected to settle in the fertile plains of the Danube or between the hills and peaks of Carinthia, Styria and the Tyrol.

EARLY WINE-DRINKING CIVILISATIONS

It was the Celts who, around the middle of the fourth century BC, first began to cultivate the vine in the region. Earlier this century archaeologists, working on the Celtic Hallstadt civilisation, discovered evidence of a developed wine-drinking culture, destroyed only once the Danubian provinces fell to the Roman occupation in 16BC (see Paul Triebaumer, p 80).

Once resistance from the Celts had ceased, the Romans settled down to administering the region; introducing their own practices and customs and paying homage to their own wine deities. Bacchus was venerated in the ancestors of Austria's cities and evidence of his cult has been found in Poetivio (Pettau) and Celeia (Cilli). Poetivio was known in Roman times as an important trading centre for wine and a local centre for barrel manufacture.

Wine was an integral part of Roman life, and it followed that vines would be planted in the wake of the conquest. Recent Austrian writers have compared the Roman use of wine to the heyday of the British Empire when, far from home and in ever more unusual climates, British families still sat

The Roman triumphal arch at Carnuntum.

down at 4pm for tea. Just as the waterways of France and Germany began to reflect the terraces of grapes planted along their banks, so the Danube was to be framed by steep rows of vines. In the south of modern Austria, Styria was soon producing wines of a quality which allowed them to be transported to Rome itself.

The wines themselves were often 'improved' by the addition of honey, pepper or spices. As an indication of their value, locals were prepared to exchange a young slave for an amphora of wine.

In the history of European viticulture, much has been made of the famous Edict of Domitian of 92AD, which prohibited the planting of vines. Whether the decree was actually enacted is open to question, especially if one is to believe the following passage from the historian Suetonius:

"One year, when a bumper vintage followed a poor grain harvest, Domitian concluded that the cornlands were being neglected in favour of the vineyards. He therefore issued an edict that forbade the further planting of vines in Italy, and ordered the acreage in the provinces to be reduced by at least half, if it could not be got rid of altogether, yet he took no steps to implement this edict."

As history has frequently demonstrated, decrees of this sort are almost impossible to enforce, and it is quite likely that a large amount of Austria's vineyards remained intact. Whatever the case, however, Austrian writers and winemakers have never been slow to pay homage to one of Domitian's successors: the Emperor Probus (276–282AD).

Probus had begun life as a simple soldier who had defeated an important thrust of the barbarian invasions which were then threatening the Empire. Possibly realising the danger of keeping a large army idle, Probus repealed Domitian's edict in 280AD, specifically mentioning the Pannonian plains to the east of modern Austria, along with Gaul as the area to be planted: "*Probus Gallos et Pannonios vineas habere permissit.*" The Emperor went further, he actually sent in the army to help out with his first-ever *furie du planteur*. Clearly Probus' action benefited much more than just the Pannonian plains: "Probus enabled the vine to resume its march to the north." (Dr Franz Leskoschek, 1934.)

Left: A view of Krems across the Danube from Mautern. Below: The Weinschlössl, Dürnstein, now part of the Freie Weingärtner Cooperative.

Probus proposed, the barbarians disposed. The vines of Austria, encouraged by Probus, were all but destroyed by the successive waves of invasion which swept across the Hungarian *Puszta* (Pannonian plain) towards Italy and the west. In the vacuum occasioned by the Romans' flight, Lower Austria was settled by the same Langobardi, or Lombards, who gave their name to the Italian province to the north of the Po. The Lombards continued to make wine, but their sites were rarely the same as those of the Romans. Historical continuity was maintained only in the rarest of cases.

THE NEW VIGNOBLES

It was the defeat of the Magyars at the Battle of Lechfeld in 955 which, at last, opened up Styria and the Danubian provinces to a new *furie du planteur*. But whereas the agents of Probus' spree had been out-of-work soldiers, the new lords of the vines were the Bavarian monasteries which followed Charlemagne's armies of liberation.

The Bavarian monasteries were richly endowed institutions founded in the course of the ninth and tenth centuries, frequently by Irish missionaries. Their first Lower Austrian creation was the *Stift* (abbey) Göttweig, perched high above the Danube opposite the city of Krems. Göttweig was to set a

precedent for the creation of vineyards along this reach of the Danube, opening up the Wachau to colonisation by the vine. By the end of the Middle Ages 42 monasteries possessed vineyards in and around Krems, and a substantial number of daughter houses had been founded along the river banks. Many of these were dissolved by the reforming Emperor Joseph II in 1792. Two notable examples of monastic institutions which have now become major secular wine producers are the Freie Weingärtner Cooperative in Dürnstein (*see p* 48) and Erich Salomon's Undhof estate in Und (*see p* 54). The Kloster Und (*see p* 54), now one of Austria's leading wine museums and vinothèques, is another former monastery which was disbanded by Joseph II.

One more vineyard which testifies to Lower Austria's emergence from the turmoils of the Dark Ages was that of Gumpoldskirchen. As one might expect, it was one Gumpold, bishop of the proselytizing Bavarian see of Passau, who endowed the church in about the year 900. A part of the grant was the vines on the hillsides, the income from which was intended to support the upkeep of church, priest and parish.

German colonists reached Burgenland on the edge of the Pannonian Plain before the end of the ninth century, and they must have planted what were possibly the first new vineyards since Probus' time. Charlemagne granted the colonists the right to the first ever *Buschenschenken*: inns where a vineyard owner has the right to sell his own wine for a limited number of days per year. Burgenland remained a German-speaking area, even though it was soon to revert to the Hungarian crown. As in Lower Austria, the monks proved the greatest innovators in the vineyards. The monastery at Güssing was founded in 1157 by the Cistercian order from Burgundy's Côte d'Or. They brought with them their own grapes, the burgundian Pinot Gris or Ruländer. The locals, associating the newcomer with the tonsured gentlemen who set such store by the wine, baptised the grape the *Grauer Mönch*, or Grey Monk.

It was the Hungarian King Imre who created the reputation of the wine towns of Rust and Ödenburg (the modern Hungarian town of Sopron), when in 1203 he granted the Cistercians of the Abbey of Heiligenkreuz a strip of land bordering the northern shores of the Neusiedlersee. In the centuries to follow the monks had plenty of time to observe the beneficial effects of the autumnal mists which, year in year out, rose from the shallow lake, infecting the grapes with *Botrytis cinerea* (noble rot).

Heiligenkreuz was one of three monastic foundations started by the Austrian national saint, Margrave Leopold (1073–1136). The other two were the Benedictine monastery of Mariazell and the great abbey of Klosterneuburg, a few miles to the west of Vienna. It was at Klosterneuburg that Saint Leopold's bones were finally laid, giving the monastery a status which it has retained to this day. Then and now, Klosterneuburg possessed vineyards throughout Lower Austria, including some of the best sites in the Viennese hills on the slopes of Nussdorf, Weidling, Grinzing and Klosterneuburg itself.

The same process of monastic or ecclesiastical colonisation accounted for the planting of vines in Styria. The Cistercians played their part there too with their foundations at Rein and Reuntale-bei-Grafwein. At Gross-Sonntag the warlike Teutonic Knights owned vines, presumably used to provision their soldiers busy with the Christian conquest of the Baltic. After the monks came the Bishops of Seckau, Salzburg, Lavant and Gurk, each owning vineyards in the area. In Styria, the spread of Christianity had great bearing on the growth of vineyard land. Given that there was ten times the present area under vine, consumption within and without the monasteries must have been very high.

Above: A baroque Bürgerhaus *in the free city of Rust.*
Right: The vineyard in Schwarzenbergplatz, Vienna. A wine was made here in 1991.

Vines belonging to the wine school in Klosterneuburg.

By the eleventh and twelfth centuries Austria was exporting wine all over Europe. Barrels of Viennese and Krems wine found their way not only to the neighbouring provinces of Bohemia and Moravia (in the present Czecho-Slovakia), but also to north Germany, the Baltic States and even England. The profitability of the still largely monastic vineyards must have appealed to successive Austrian rulers as endowments followed thick and fast. In 1141, for example, Duke Leopold V granted further vineyards to the Abbey of Heiligenkreuz, and his successor, Duke Heinrich Fasomirgott endowed Mariazell with another site 15 years later. In the year 1200 Leopold VII made a present of a vineyard to the hospital in Passau.

It is not always clear whether or not this largesse on the part of the Austrian rulers was intended for monastic consumption or pecuniary gain. With Friedrich der Streitbare's (Frederick the Pugnacious) decree of 1231 allowing Klosterneuburg

to send 15 *Fuder* (tuns) of wine annually to the town of Enns, however, the purpose becomes clear. Klosterneuburg was to add to its already considerable wealth accumulated from the profits from its vineyards in Grinzing and the like. In 1328 Heiligenkreuz was allowed to sell wine in the markets of Bruck, Marchegg, Wiener Neustadt and Vienna.

Hand in hand with the fight to control export markets came protection for the home market. In 1364 Lower Austria was forbidden territory to salesmen bringing consignments of 'foreign' wine. As in other European cities such as Bordeaux, Vienna's *bourgeois* were granted their own wine privilege whereby only they had the entitlement to sell wine within the city limits. As in Bordeaux, this rule was relaxed between Martinmass and Christmas, when the *vignerons* of Lower Austria had the right to sell their wines in the market.

Most of these privileged Viennese burghers possessed *Buschenschenken*, or taverns, where their wines were sold in warm rooms offering good food to draw the customers in. The vineyards which supplied these drinking dens were not only up in the hills to the west of the city, some were within the walls themselves, like those at the Kärntnertor (near the present opera house), the Schottentor, Ottakring and by the Minoritenkirche. A last vestige of these inner-city vineyards can still be seen behind a balustrade in the Schwarzenbergplatz, where 19 vines are still mysteriously tended year in year out, only so that their fruit can be scrumped, unripe, by teams of local schoolchildren.

Those same schoolchildren might have been deterred by the draconian laws enacted in 1352 to prevent just such a thing. Grape-stealers were liable to have their ears cut off, while the modest crime of laziness during the vintage was rewarded by the amputation of a hand. Despite these horrendous punishments, Vienna appears to have been a merry place in the fifteenth century, at least if the poet Hofmann is to be believed:

> *Froheit hat genommen überhand*
> *Und allermeist in Österland*
> *Trunken, voll und nimmer Satt*
> *Ist mancher Mann in Wiener Stadt.*
> *Und etliche Fraue auch all da.*

> Merriment has the upper hand
> Especially in Austria's land
> Drinking, stuffing – always swilling,
> Vienna's menfolk, ever willing,
> And their women, too.

While Hofmann was writing these verses on the quality of life in Vienna, the town of Rust was beginning a meteoric rise which was to bring it fame and fortune over the next three centuries. By 1470, the reputation of its wines had pushed the King of Hungary* to grant the town a market. By 1542, Ruster wine had become such a valuable commodity that the king granted a *Markenschutz* (trademark) allowing barrels to be branded with the

letter R. The corks of Ruster wines are branded with the letter R to this day.

The mention of Rust leads ineluctably to discussion of the *Ausbruch* wines which became its chief claim to fame. It is hard to speak of these now rare wines, made from a mixture of nobly rotten and a small amount of healthy grapes, without bringing up that most famous of Hungarian wines, Tokay. Tokay takes its name from the region in the northwest of the country. Both Rust and Tokay trace their origins back to the early Middle Ages but only later became established as producers of great wines, Tokay. It is worth noting the basic difference between these two wines: *Ausbruch* from Rust is made by adding fresh grapes to the nobly-rotten grape must in order to activate fermentation. In Tokay, *Ausbruch*, or *Aszú* in Hungarian, is made by adding the must of nobly-rotten grapes to a base Tokay wine. One of the most important sources for the history of Tokay is a book published in 1800 by a Herr von Szirmay, a member of one of Tokay's noble dynasties, and titled *Noticia topographica politica inclyti Comitatus Zempliniensis*. In his book, Szirmay makes it clear that mediaeval growers had not possessed the secret of making *Ausbruch* wines. There was no doubting the quality, however, as is shown by the following story about the local primate, the Archbishop of Kalotsa who attended the ecumenical Council of Trent in 1562. The Archbishop had brought with him some of his best wine and had the courtesy to send a glass up to the table of Pope Pius IV. According to Franz Schams, a Hungarian oenologist, the Pope found the wine so excellent that, glass in hand, he slurped up the last few drops and cried out that such wines should be drunk only by Popes.

However good the wine must have tasted to Pius IV, it was not yet what is now called *Ausbruch*. As Franz Schams observed in 1832, the date for the first Tokay *Ausbruch* must have been about a century later. It was at about this time "that in Tokay and the surrounding region, people began to look after the wines with greater care, to plough the vineyards three times a year and put off the harvest till late in the autumn, setting aside the dry berries" (Schams). In 1655 the picking of these *Trockenbeeren* was still a novelty, and the local peasants were not a bit happy about the greater work-load it

---

* Rust did not become part of Austria until 1921, when it was decided to heed the lamentations of the German-speaking majority who had been assigned to Hungary under the terms of the Treaty of Saint-Germain.

Muskat Lunel grapes affected by Botrytis cinerea.

Furmint grapes; formerly the mainstay of Ruster Ausbruch.

involved. The peasants worked to rule, and the overlords brought the case before the courts. The judges however, sided with the workers and decreed that "the number of dry berries to be collected must be limited" (Schams).

At that time grape varieties used in Tokay and Rust seem to have been much the same. For the great sweet wines the favourite was the Furmint, known as the Zapfner or Zapfnete in Rust, and the Ordinäre (clearly no rarety) in Güns (now Köszeg) to the south of the lake. There is no watertight evidence that Rust was making *Ausbruch* wines any earlier than Tokay, but given the climatic conditions around the Neusiedlersee, noble rot would have quite naturally occurred in any late-picked vintage. The Zapfner was already deemed the most important of Rust's cultivars in 1634. Fifteen years later the emperor absolved the locals from the feudal dues in recognition of the quality of the wine. In 1681 the town was enobled as an Imperial Free City. Disaster came the following year in the form of a plague of locusts, which continued to ravage the vineyards until 1693. In 1683 there was the even more famous plague of Turks on their way to besiege Vienna. Despite all these calamities, *Ruster Ausbruch* had already become a highly sought-after commodity in Silesia, Thorn, Danzig, Königsberg and Riga.

It would seem that these two wines came into existence within a few years of one another. Which came first is hard to say. Where Tokay had the advantage over Rust was in the fact that noble rot occurred more regularly there than on the Neusied-

lersee, and that the cellars of the Carpathian Mountains had the advantage of dryness, thereby giving rise to flor bacteria which impart the special sherry-like flavours associated with Tokay. In the course of the eighteenth century Tokay went from strength to strength and by the following century the world had virtually forgotten about Rust's existence. Perhaps it was for this reason that after the final scourge of phylloxera, *Ruster Ausbruch* virtually ceased to be made.

Across the border in Lower Austria it was still believed necessary to protect ordinary people from winemakers who planted grapes rather than other (edible) crops. In 1417 the ruling duke enforced a Domitian-style edict which prohibited the planting of vines; most likely growers paid as little attention to him as they did to the Roman Emperor. In order to protect the growers in turn from foreign competition, Hungarian wines were banned in 1453 and in 1539 those of Moravia and Bohemia were denied access to Austrian markets. By this time there was little need to worry about competition from Hungary, which had fallen to the Sultan's armies. In 1529, the Turks reached the gates of Vienna for the first of two memorable sieges.

A TOPER'S PARADISE

When it comes to the quality of Austrian wine at the end of the sixteenth century there is much to be gleaned from the *Weinbuch* written in 1582 by Johann Rasch. Rasch offers a wealth of detail, dividing Lower Austria into five main regions, at the centre of which lay Vienna, which was still considered to produce the best wines within the duchy. The Viennese themselves clearly thought most highly of it, as consumption within the city at the time has been estimated at 120 litres per head. Needless to say, drunkenness was common.

The authorities continued to play a game of cat and mouse with the growers for the next 200 years. The trade was freed in 1602 but further attempts were made to prevent planting in the eighteenth century. Despite these measures, the area planted with vines actually increased steadily throughout the century. In 1683 the Turks were once again at the gates of Vienna. The failure of the siege had a number of lasting effects on Vienna. For one, it introduced the inhabitants to coffee, when a consignment of discarded beans was discovered after the city was relieved by the armies of Jan Sobieski. This was to start a love-affair between the citizens and the beverage which has survived undiminished into our own time. Another innovation borne out of the siege was the croissant, made by Viennese bakers in imitation of the crescent moon on the Turkish standards. The Turks retreated into Hungary, whence they were ejected by the forces of Prince Eugene of Savoy over the next 25 years. Only one Ottoman remained, the legendary Purbach Turk who, stopping in Purbach on his way to the siege, got so drunk that he was left behind.

DER PURBACHER TÜRKE

War das ein Wein!
Geträumt?
Wo bin ich nur?
Der siebte Himmel kann's nicht sein,
Ich hör' doch Christenhunde schrei'n
Nicht ein Spur
Von meinem Haufen.
Verdammtes Saufen

Jetzt tränk ich erst den Brunnen leer.
Die Beine ziehn wie Blei.
Das ist mein Schädel auch nicht mehr!
* – Und das Geschrei! –*
Der Rauchfang, der ist frei,
Will drin verschnaufen.
Verdammtes Saufen.

Ich müsste eigentlich nach Wien,
Mein Aller – ha,
Der stellt mich an der Wand.
Und hier verreck' ich im Kamin.
Bin so und so dann hin.
Hilf, Allah – Diese Schand!
Könnt ich nur laufen.
Verdammtes Saufen.

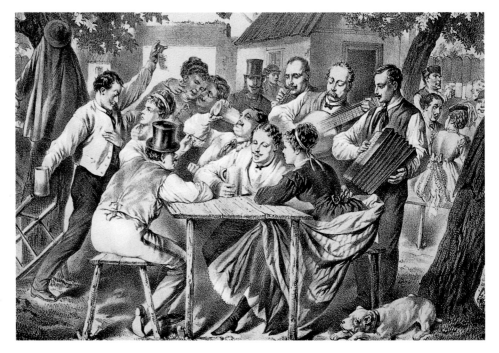

A 19th-century Heurige *scene. Since the 19th century the* Heurigen *have provided the Viennese with country inns offering cheap, wholesome food and wine made on the premises.*

Die heizen ein. Das hat gefehlt.
Es geht nur übers Dach.
Gut zwanzig hab ich schon gezählt.
Allein bin ich zu schwach,
Und Allah hilft nicht noch.
Ach was,
Ich lass mich taufen,
Verdammtes Saufen.

War das ein Wein!
Der Halbmond grinst herein.

Eugen Mayer

So that was wine!
Or else, a dream?
What is this place?
Not seventh heaven – I can tell!
I hear those dogs of Christians yell!
And of my men there's not a trace
My troop I'll lose:
Oh, cursed booze!

Just now I drank the fountain dry
My legs feel made of lead
And this can't really be my head
Oh, how those Christians cry!
I'll climb into the chimney breast
And take a snooze.
Oh, cursed booze!

Vienna's where I *should* have gone,
His Excellencal – ah,
Despatched me to besiege the town
But here I am, by hook or crook,
Stuck half way up the ingle-nook
Allah – don't let me down!
Show me a ruse!
O cursed booze!

They've lit the fire. I've made a blunder.
And so the roof's the only way:
There must be 20 men, by thunder,
And only one of me.
Allah – too late
At any rate
It's baptism I choose!
O cursed booze!

So that was wine!
And Allah must resign.

An inn in Purbach commemorating the Purbach Turk.

With the departure of all but the Purbach Turk went the menace of invasion which had hung over Lower Austria for nearly two centuries. It now meant that the city could open out towards the hills and vineyards to the West. This had the effect of encouraging the growth of the *Buschenschenken* in the villages of Grinzing, Weidling and Nussdorf. A greater freedom governed the harvest in the Viennese vineyards where the vintage took as many as 40 days to finish with the help of up to 1,200 horses.

With the newly relaxed atmosphere in the city, there was more time to admire the quality of the local brews. In the eighteenth century the Viennese wines had their own hierarchy of *crus* and the cognoscenti allowed them to age for 20 years or so before broaching the cask. The proximity of these famous vineyards to the seat of the court was a point which struck successive generations of visitors to the imperial capital: "Few, indeed no other court, has the good fortune to have so many of Bacchus' blessings, so close at hand, so fine and so plentiful." (Franz Schams, 1835.)

The marked supremacy of Grinzing, Weidling and Nussdorf over the other *crus* led to wine snobbery on a scale reminiscent only of Bordeaux during the same period. Towards the end of the eighteenth century some Viennese wine lovers decided to do a test in order to find out which of the three was indeed the best. After a particularly good harvest a cask of each was set aside in the same cellar. The wines were treated with exactly the same minute care, racked and maintained until the time was deemed right to taste them at their best. When the moment came, the debate was agonised,

In der Schenke *by Nader,*
Wiener Historischer Museum.

but finally the Grinzing won the day, except that, as the chronicler of the event tells us: "although it was the best wine, it was overmatched by the spicy palate of the Weidling".

The most famous wine of the Habsburg empire, however, was still without a doubt Tokay. In 1779 the Empress Maria Theresa promulgated a new order governing the sale of the wines and their manufacture. Her reforming son Joseph II followed up with his own decrees five years later, setting a tax on *Ausbruch* wines which, one assumes, also included those of Rust. There was considerable fraud involved in the creation of these luscious wines, which had become a *sine qua non* at the northern courts. An order of 1823 laid down a scale of penalties for those caught making Tokay from a concoction of honey, sugar and raisins; a sleight of hand which recalls a time nearer to our own.

Joseph II was also a reformer of the *Buschenschenken*, laying down the still largely applicable rules for the sale of food to go with the wine. Joseph decided that the bread served must be baked on the premises, and the pigs too must be the family pigs, slaughtered on the premises. In around 1800 the word *Heurige* first came to be used to describe the Viennese *Buschenschenken*. The word has come to mean all at once the establishment and the fresh young wines from the promiscuous vineyards behind the vat-house.

The French Revolution and its aftermath took its toll on Austria's wines. One victim was the great monastery of Klosterneuburg, where Napoleon blew up the cellars containing vintages going back hundreds of years. The wines had been used for the sick – the theory being that old wine was a medicine for fatigue. The only wine artefact to survive the Corsican's destructive urge was the great tun of the monastery. When the wars came to an end in 1815, the oldest wines in the cellar were those of the legendary comet-year: 1811. History repeated itself in 1945, when Russian soldiers drank the massive monastery cellars dry.

The French invasions of 1805 and 1809 laid waste to the vineyards. The Battle of Wagram, which sealed Austria's defeat in 1809, was actually fought over one of Lower Austria's choicest sites.

Conscription meant that there were few men left to tend the vines or work in the cellars. This, and a series of poor harvests from 1813 to 1817, encouraged growers to rethink their approach to their business. By the time the battle of Waterloo had finally removed Napoleon from Europe and stowed him out of harm's way in the middle of the Atlantic, wine consumption in Vienna had dwindled to 87 litres per head. If this hardly designates a sober city, it nonetheless points to a sharp decline since the sixteenth century.

POST-WATERLOO PROGRESS

Adversity is the mother of progress. Almost as soon as the Napoleonic Wars came to an end, Austrian winemakers found the means to improve their wines. The first thing to tackle was the basis of wine production: grapes. Wine nurseries came into fashion when, in 1817, Franz Ritter von Heintl, an enlightened estate owner, managed to assemble a collection of all the vines in the Habsburg Empire. In 1819 one Hofrat von Görög went one better. On his land in Grinzing, Görög founded a nursery, as one contemporary gushed, ". . . not of the Austrian imperial lands alone. No! a grape nursery of the whole world!" Görög's collection was certainly impressive: it listed 565 French varieties, 453 from the Empire, 257 from Venice, 48 from Milan, 48 from Dalmatia, 45 from Sicily, 32 from Ragusa, 30 from Florence, 20 from Tripoli, 13 from Naples, and 6 from Smyrna. Görög died in 1833 and his prodigious collection of vines appears to have followed him to the grave soon after.

Meanwhile, Paul Ludwig von Conrad, another estate owner, started to analyse the vineyards of Rust. In his book *Beschreibung des Ruster Weinbaues* of 1819, Conrad details the immense care which went into the selection of grapes for the *Ausbruch* wines: the successive pickings; the anxieties concerning weather too warm early in the year and the importance of the *Kochmonat* (the cooking month), August, and the *Gewürzmonat* (spice month), September, in the ripening of the fruit. From Heintl we learn of the immense care to prevent the oxidisation of the wines in the barrel; adding washed pebbles to the casks to maintain the

The Augustinian monastery and town of Klosterneuburg.

level of the wine and keep out the damaging air.

Furmint was still the staple grape variety for *Ausbruch*. Other cultivars, like the Hungarian grape Augsterrebe and the generally poor-quality Griechische (the Greek), went to make up the second-rate wines destined for local consumption. There was also a fair amount of the then ubiquitous Silberweisse, as well as some of the Thermenregion's Zierfandler. Conrad had no high opinion of the Zierfandler, calling it "sweet, but without other qualities". It is perhaps surprising, considering the generally late development of botrytised wines in France, to see how soon the Tokayers and Rusters understood the importance of autumnal mists in creating their luscious wines. The beneficial nature of the autumn fog is well described by the nineteenth-century Viennese poet Johann Nepomuk Vogl in this touching poem:

DER NEBEL

Der Nebel sich herniedersenkt,
Der Nebel in dem Weinberg hängt,
Und jede Traube trinkt daran,
Soviel sie kann.

Das eben freut den Winzer sehr,
Da gibt es Wein um desto mehr,
Ein Nebel zu seiner Zeit
Ist sehr gescheit.

Mir aber wird es plötzlich klar,
Was mir so lang ein Rätsel war,
Woher es: dass man kann vom Wein
Vernebelt sein.

THE MIST

This mist sinks down and rests among
The vineyards now so richly hung
With thirsty grapes which lap
All they can tap.

It makes the grower, too, rejoice,
It makes his wine that much more choice,
A mist which falls when due.
No man should rue.

And suddenly I see dissolve.
The riddle I could not resolve:
How once a man his wine has tried,
He's mystified.

We are well informed as to the state of Austria's vineyards in the post-Waterloo years through the writings of pioneering Austrian and Hungarian oenologists. The best of these was the Hungarian Franz Schams whose three-volume work on the wines of the Monarchy, *Der Weinbau des Oesterreichischen Kaiser-Staates in seinem ganzen Umfange*, was published between 1832 and 1835. As a guide it has few equals, even in contemporary France.

Schams was naturally also interested in the phenomena of Tokay and Rust. Unlike earlier writers he had taken the trouble to visit both places, and knew how Rust's shallow lake affected the microclimate differently from the River Bodrog. He writes that "the air in the vicinity of the lake is gentle and warm, and as a result of the constant evaporation, soft." Furthermore, the climate by the lakeside is warmer than that of the surrounding hills. When the snow lies thick on the ground in Eisenstadt, the shores of the Neusiedlersee can be bone dry. There is consequently less danger from late frost and the grapes develop early: berries are forming while in the hills only buds are visible.

The local tradition was to prune early "*auf den Schnee schneiden*" (prune in the snow), in order to ensure the longest possible growing season. The harvest in Rust was the latest in the Monarchy, even later than that of Tokay, beginning usually around 28 October. This was to ensure that the greatest number of overripe bunches would be picked. In the best years the vintage continued for six weeks: "the people of Rust often continue their vintage into the month of December when there is no longer a leaf to be seen on the vines", says Schams; "the bunches are either shrivelled or dried out. Grapes fall to the ground or are wrenched from the bunches by the wind, so that the pickers must select their grapes in the most rigorous sense of the word."

As the stalks dried out, one team of pickers would collect the dry berries, while others followed behind taking bunches of a lesser quality. Schams' next contention is of vital importance in understanding the historical nature of these famous sweet Hungarian wines as they existed in the heyday of

Rust, the free city on the shores of the shallow Niesiedlersee. In the foreground, Blaufränkisch vines.

the Austrian Empire. There is still considerable confusion on this score among writers, and few winemakers in the Burgenland are wholly clear as to what the situation used to be. New Austrian laws, such as those promulgated in 1972 and 1985, not only created German-style *Prädikat* categories like *Auslese*, *Beerenauslese*, and *Trockenbeerenauslese*, which did not formerly exist in Austria; they also to some degree paraphrased the process which had been used to make *Ausbruch*. "The first dried berries picked yield the so-called 'essence', writes Schams; "which, along with the partially dry-berried bunches (*Trockenbeeren untermengte Trauben*), produce the *Ausbruch*. The last passage through the vines brings in all the remaining bunches which are used to make the ordinary wines of Rust, which are, this notwithstanding, excellent drinks."

As is the case in modern Tokay, the grapes were pressed separately in small presses. The *Trockenbeeren* lacking moisture formed a slimy mass rather than a must proper. Quantities of this jelly were then added to the must derived from the bunches of only partially nobly rotten fruit, or vice versa. This meant that *Ausbruch* was a blend of *Trockenbeerenauslese* and late-picked wine. In an exceptional vintage the latter would have been at *Beerenauslese* level, in a less-favoured one, more like *Spätlese*. Similarly, the ordinary wine spoken of by Schams would have been as good as *Auslese* in top vintages and increasingly 'ordinaire' when no noble rot occurred on the vines. The present confusion has been largely created by the growers reserving their best berries for their bottles of German-style *Trockenbeerenauslese*.

More enlightened contemporary growers in Rust believe that the only major difference which existed between the *Ausbruch* of Tokay and Rust lay in the absence of any systematic addition of butts of *Trockenbeeren* pulp in Rust, because they did not see *Botrytis cinerea* every year.

The period following the Napoleonic wars proved a boom time in Rust. The chief customers for the wines were merchants from Silesia and Poland who scoured the lakeside cellars, their pockets filled with ducats. These were the middlemen who sold on the wine to devotees in Northern Europe and the Baltic Principalities. A small quan-

tity even reached the British Isles and Pennsylvania in the United States. In London it was tasted by the surgeon and prototype wine-writer Alexander Henderson. Henderson had written to Schams in Pest, telling him that Rust wine was so good that "every drop must be savoured to the last".

South of the Neusiedlersee in Central Burgenland a high proportion of the grapes grown were black. With a fair dollop of Hungarian national pride, Schams compares the wines favourably with those of Burgundy. "Some people", he tells us, "even prefer them (to those of) the Côte d'Or! If not quite the king, at least the joint regent of French wines." The grapes involved at the time were the Blauer Zierfandler and the Schwarzer Muskateller. It is not clear whether either of these are synonyms for the now prevalent Blaufränkisch.

The luscious sweet wines and beefy reds of the

Left: The completed corner of the 'Escorial' at Klosterneuburg.
Below: Schotterboden: gravelly, red-wine soils in Tattendorf.

Burgenland belonged properly to Hungary. Across the border in Lower Austria most of the wines were light and white with an "insignificant" percentage of red wines coming from the Südbahn to the south of the capital. If Lower Austria lacked the variety associated with Hungarian wines, the overall standard was good: "Austrian white wines belong indisputably to the best table wines of the Empire and they have maintained their fame for centuries". Schams nevertheless warns his Austrian readers against resting on their laurels: much had to be done to improve quality. Then as now, Lower Austrian wines were marked out by their high acidity levels, which meant that they took a long time to mellow. A Hungarian wine was at its peak after five or six years, while Austrian wines required ageing for 15 to 20 years before they were pleasant to drink.

Austria's most famous wines were still those within easiest reach of the Imperial capital: Grinzing, Nussdorf, Weidling and Klosterneuburg. Klosterneuburg was chiefly famed for the enormous holdings of the Augustinian monastery which, in the first years of the eighteenth century, had been designated to become an Austrian Escorial: palace and royal monastery rolled into one. The chief grape of the Viennese vineyards was the Grobe, a cultivar which seems to have died out in all but a few patches in the Wachau. Schams spoke highly of it, adding that in "earlier times it was more widespread that it is now". It was a late-ripener, which had made it increasingly unpopular, and it was being steadily replaced by more light-sensitive white grapes. Here and there was a spot of Riesling and a little Grüner Muskateller; the latter was the forerunner of Grüner Veltliner.

South of Vienna was the Thermenregion, or Südbahn. On the gravelly soils of Tattendorf and Bad Vöslau experiments had been successfully carried out planting black grapes: "Here we find an area where even from some distance we can see the blue (*sic*) grapes which, though they rarely make an appearance on the market, actually make a quality drink, especially in favourable years such as 1834 when fully ripened grapes come to their aid."

The grapes in question were the Blauburgunder (Pinot Noir) and the Blauer Portugieser. Schams also mentions a Schwarzfränkisch which was known in Vöslau as the Mährisch or Moravian

Gumpoldskirchen. The church founded by Bishop Gumpold of Passau. Traditionally Gumpoldskirchen specialises in sweet wines.

grape (an indication of its origin?); this was almost certainly the Blaufränkisch, now more widely grown in Burgenland. Blaufränkisch did not fare well on the region's gravel and with time it was the Blauer Portugieser which won out against the later ripening Pinot Noir. Schams was under the impression that the Portugieser was a Spanish variety(!). This is unlikely. The probable origin of the grape is Hungary.

Schams was at pains to show how recent these red-wine experiments had been: "Vöslau reds are a product of modern times. At a rough calculation they must have existed for about 30 years, and have always sold at a higher price than the whites."

The Hungarian was not impressed by the wines of the nearby spa town of Baden and recommends that visitors stick to the water. At Pfaffstätten, the property of the all-powerful Cistercian monastery of Heiligenkreuz, he admired the new tendency to plant vines in orderly rows, thereby facilitating ploughing, tending and picking. In most regions of Austria the growers still adhered to the mediaeval method of planting grapes willy-nilly. Bordeaux had phased this practice out at the end of the seventeenth century.

On the hills of Gumpoldskirchen the land was deemed more suitable for white wine production. Most of the vineyards were "promiscuous", yield-

ing the so-called *gemischter Satz*, a blend of all grapes which is still popular in *Heurigen*. This method presented a problem in Gumpoldskirchen, with its warm microclimate, as the grapes tended to ripen at widely varying times. In the 1830s efforts were being made to isolate the best cultivars; the result was that the *Gumpoldskirchner*, or Roter Zierfandler, achieved a greater popularity. The Zierfandler was already responsible for the "special flavour" of Gumpoldskirchen wines. Schams also found a quantity of Riesling being grown in the vineyards, with the best wines coming from the experimental estates of Counts Haugwitz and Harrach. Harrach had also planted Pinot Noir in a plot behind his *Schloss*.

Until the recent wine scandal, Gumpolskirchen was famous for its sweet wines. The main street of the small town was (and is) one long line of *Heurigen*, which during the summer months were crammed to bursting point with sweet-toothed Germans and more recently Japanese. In the 1830s, however, sweet wine production was still in its infancy in the region, with a few growers trying to make imitations of the wines of Rust. When no *Botrytis cinerea* appeared in the hills, some growers made *Strohweine* (straw wine) resembling the *vins de paille* occasionally made in the French Jura or in Hermitage on the Rhône: ". . . here vineyard owners can be observed practising the praise-worthy manoeuvre of plucking berries from their vines to make a better wine in years when the grapes do not achieve sufficient ripeness [this is called a *vendange verte* in French]. Also, in the best years, attempts have been made to produce *Ausbruch* here. To this end bunches are laid out on house floors or hung up on strings to dry.''

The other traditional grape of the Südbahn is the Rotgipfler, which Schams found growing in the villages of Mödling, Thallern and Mauer. In Mauer (now in the 23rd Bezirk – or district – of Vienna) Schams identified Riesling grapes growing alongside the Rotgipfler. The growers of Mauer, he reports, had hit upon an interesting new technique to ensure that their wines sold well on the unquenchable Viennese market: fermentation in new oak barrels. ''The people of Mauer are of the peculiar opinion that the wine is much better when it is fermented in new barrels, and they are careful to add that the higher selling price is ample compensation for the outlay on new casks. Although I have no doubt as to the veracity of this assertion, as many years of experience have led these people to their conclusions, I am quite unable to clarify what beneficial influence the wines might derive from the process of having their alcoholic fermentation take place in new oak barrels.'' Finally, Schams reserves judgement until he has tried out the process in his vineyard in Pest.

To the west of Vienna, in the region now called Donauland-Carnuntum, Schams found the dominant grape to be the Roter Muskateller, or Roter Veltliner. Today it is rare, but one or two *vignerons* – notably Sepp Mantler in Kamptal-Donauland – still make a little wine from it with interesting results. Schams was not taken with the wines of the Roter Muskateller, which he sampled on the battle-field of Wagram and in the villages of Riedenthal, Ottenthal and Neudegg. He adds that the growers might have been better off with the Bohemian Printsch grape (the Weisser Burgunder or Pinot Blanc), but that they were stubbornly clinging to their old ways with the Roter Muskateller or the Grobe: ''Here they maintain the conviction that the Grobe is the best of grapes, even when experience has taught them the opposite.'' In the years 1813 to 1833, the Grobe had frequently rotted on the vines.

Further to the west in Krems, Schams sampled the local speciality: gin. This gin, which was more like a vermouth flavoured with Moravian juniper berries, was at this period extremely popular in Bavaria and Poland (one assumes that, for the Poles to enjoy it, it must have been high in alcohol). It was formerly an important source of prosperity for Krems. No trace of Kremser gin exists today.

The Grobe was once again the favoured grape in the Wachau (where today they will tell you that, somewhere near a small local stream called the Ritzling, the Riesling was born). Although Schams admired the wines, and those of Weissenkirchen in particular, he thought the Grobe a liability: ''In good years this cultivar makes a good wine. In bad years it makes good vinegar.'' (Johann Rasch had rhymed ''*Sauer wie die Wachauer*'' – sour like Wachau wine.) Schams found the Wachau population to be unshakeable in their faith in the Grobe, dismissing all other grape varieties as ''foreigners''. A local oenologist by the name of Dechater was fighting a battle to the death to get the *encépagement* changed. Schams believed the solution would have been to plant Pinot Blanc, Gewürztraminer or the Hungarian Honigtraube. He made no mention of Riesling, which since the Second World War has shown itself perfectly adapted to the steep terraces overlooking the Danube.

Weissenkirchen, one of the Wachau villages along the Danube.

In 1835 Langenlois was "one of the best wine towns in Austria . . . without a break, the whole area under vine resembles a green carpet." Local industry proved an insatiable market for the wines made from both Grüner and Roter Muskateller. The Grüner Muskateller was probably the Grüner Veltliner, now Austria's most widely planted grape, accounting for as much as a third of the area under vine. Schams believed the best wines of Kamptal-Donauland came from the villages of Kammern and Zöbing, where the soil was volcanic.

In the Weinviertel, near the pretty fortified town of Eggenburg and the village of Röschitz, Schams found growers wholly won over to the Grüner Muskateller. The same process of colonisation was taking place in the Pulkau Valley, where the Grüner Muskateller was taking over from the Roter Zierfandler and the Riesling. Only in Markersdorf and two other villages had the old grape varieties survived, and these were still responsible for producing the best wines in the valley. Pulkau is now better known for red wines made from the Blauer Portugieser and the modern Blauburger cross.

The secret of the Grüner Muskateller's progress had been the belief that the old grapes, including the Rhine Riesling, had been tough and slow to mature. Schams, however, reminds us of a Hungarian saying that "a tough wine is not a bad wine". In Untermarkersdorf, Schams proves that the Grüner Muskateller was indeed the Grüner Veltliner: "As in all places the nomenclature given to grape varieties comes as a result of accident or caprice, so the Grüner Muskateller – that universally treasured grape – is here called the Weissgipfler, because the tender stalks have a whitish appearance." According to the great nineteenth-century ampelographer Hermann Goethe, the Weissgipfler is in fact a synonym for the Grüner Veltliner.

The one major wine-producing area of present-day Austria which Schams failed to visit was Styria. In the last century, Styria encompassed not only the province as it exists today, but also part of the state of Slovenia. The size of the province marked it out as one of the Monarchy's main wine producers. In the first half of the nineteenth century, considerable improvements were made in the sphere of viticulture as a result of the pioneering work done by the Steirischen Landwirtschaftsgesellschaft (the Styrian Agricultural Society), and the vine nursery in Graz which helped introduce grape varieties from the Rhine. Another major influence was the radical Habsburg, Archduke Johann. Among other things, Johann was possibly responsible for introducing the Chardonnay grape to the region under the name Morillon. The Styrians learned only comparatively recently that their Morillon was the same as the grape which went to make the great white wines of Burgundy.

The second quarter of the nineteenth century launched a great wave of popularity for sparkling wines made in imitation of the great wines of Champagne. Champagne look-alikes sprang up in every corner of Europe, Austria not excepted. Schams reports many Burgenland growers who had taken to selling their grapes for Sekt production. At the same time experiments were being carried out in Vienna, especially in the suburb of Döbling where the majority of Austrian *Sektkellereien* had houses over their warrens of cellars. They existed to provide the ineffably frivolous Viennese population of the mid-century with the sort of wines best suited to their needs.

Austria's leading Sekt house, Schlumberger, was founded by the south German Robert Schlumberger in 1842. Roughly contemporary is the other Viennese giant, Johann Kattus, whose *Jugendstil* (art nouveau) labels are still quaintly emblazoned with the legend "purveyors to the court" even 70 years after the court has disappeared. Schlumberger's venture also brought him recognition from the Habsburgs, and the title of *Edler* (literally, nobleman) von Goldeck. Today Schlumberger and Kattus are Austria's best-known Sekts, but in the nineteenth century, as today, there were dozens of other firms, most of which acquired their base wines in the Weinviertel among the so-called *Brünnerstrassler* vineyards which lined the main road to the now Czech city of Brno. These wines were a byword for acidity among the Viennese, but they also possessed the advantage of the sort of clean, steely fruit necessary for sparkling wine production. One famous house, that of Verderber (which means despoiler in English), was actually based in the pretty town of Retz in the Weinviertel. Today

A grotto in the cellars of the Schlumberger sparkling wine company in Döbling, created in the mid-19th century.

many of the Sekt firms have their headquarters near the town of Poysdorf.

By no means all the Sekt cellars were confined to Döbling and the Weinviertel, however, and there was even one successful company started in Nether Styria (now Slovenia) by the same Clothar Bouvier who first identified the Bouvier grape.

Besides making an Austrian contribution to the world of sparkling wine, the nineteenth century continued the process of fine honing which had begun after the Napoleonic Wars. In Gumpolds-kirchen, for example, an enlightened grower called Johann Baumgärtner performed myriad services for the wines of the Thermenregion, not least by introducing the 'noblest' grape varieties into his grape nursery in Gumpoldskirchen. These inclu-ded Rhine Riesling grapes brought back from the Rhine, Traminer (or Gewürztraminer), Ruländer (Pinot Gris), Blauburgunder (Pinot Noir), Blauer Portugieser and St Laurent.

In 1860 Austria's first viti-vinicultural school was established in Klosterneuburg in some old cloistral buildings on the initiative of the abbot, Adam Schreck. As first director of the school, Schreck installed another man from the Thermen-region, a notable wine-scholar called August Wil-helm, Freiherr von Babo, whose bust still squats somewhat inelegantly among the flowerbeds at the entrance to the school's new buildings, constructed this century on the main Klosterneuburg-Vienna road.

PHYLLOXERA, GREED AND THE TWENTIETH CENTURY

If to some degree Austria's vineyards looked set for a rosy future as they approached the fourth and final quarter of the nineteenth century, by the time the Monarchy entered the nineties it was clear that this was not to be. Phylloxera and greed were the two main contributing factors in the partial eclipse of Austria's fame as a wine-producing country, and not all the greed was a result of the decimation caused by the wine-bug. Long before phylloxera hit Rust, for example, the growers had begun to cut corners in the grape-growing and the winemaking processes in the expectation of larger profits. The Furmint grape, which had been the mainstay of *Ausbruch* wines, was wound up in favour of early-ripening, bigger-cropping cultivars. It was the same process which had led to the introduction of hedgerow-to-hedgerow Grüner Muskateller or Grüner Veltliner.

The demise of *Ausbruch* wines in Rust must have been hastened by the drying up of the Neusiedler-see, which occurred between the years 1865 and 1871. The last proper *Ausbruch* to be made before our own time was harvested at the end of 1894. Three years later the vineyards were totally destroyed. When the time came to replant in the early years of this century, the Furmint gave way to the big-cropping Welschriesling (or Italian Riesling). There was also an explosion of red-wine making in the area to the south of the lake, with the Blaufränkisch grape predominating. Burgenland reds had begun to acquire something of a reputation (which they are building up again today), and the Iron Chancellor Bismarck, had added to the region's fame by placing a biannual order with the growers of Pöttelsdorf.

Phylloxera had been first identified at Klosterneuburg in 1872. Ten years later it began to undo all Baumgärtner's good work in the Thermenregion. In 20 years it laid waste to 9,029 hectares of vines in 126 areas, destroying a quarter of all the vines in Lower Austria. If the figures for Styria and Burgenland were added to this the total would be more alarming still.

In Austria, as elsewhere in the world, the solution to the problem was to graft the European (*vitis vinifera*) vines onto American (*vitis labrusca*) rootstock. In the majority of cases this is precisely what took place in the years prior to the First World War. In some places, however, growers stopped short of grafting, simply replacing their *vinifera* plants with *labrusca*, particularly in the poorer areas of Styria and Burgenland. The people soon grew used to the characteristic flavours given by the American vines, even those of the Noah, which is reputed to cause not only imbecility if you drink large quantities of it; but is also said to be a powerful aphrodisiac. Perhaps this is the reason why the Southern Burgenlanders are so reluctant to allow the government to remove their last 23 hectares of *Uhudler* vines, as they are called. The word derives from the local name for the eagle owl, presumably because drinking the wine makes you look about as silly as the bird.

In August 1914 Austria and Germany goaded one another into unleashing a war aimed at resolving their various claims to world power. The results were, if anything, even more doleful for Austria than they were for Germany. During the war itself the vineyards predictably suffered as the flower of Austrian youth was mown down on the battlefields.

Frau Bachkönig, the 'Uhudler Queen' of Moschendorf.

In the larger cities of the Monarchy the British Naval blockade rendered food scarce. If the satirist Karl Kraus is to be believed, the cry was for Serbians' livers and Russians' kidneys as a supplement to their meagre meat intake. In the interests of patriotism, restaurants in Vienna went to absurd lengths to disguise foreign foods by banning such kitchen terminology as hors-d'oeuvres, mayonnaise, vol-au-vent, ragout, hollandaise and macaroni.

The result of four years of callous blood-letting was the Treaty of Saint-Germain. Dramatically reduced in size and importance, Austria exchanged its imperial vocation for a touristic one. Between the wars trippers swarmed over the borders to sample the famous Austrian *Gemütlichkeit* (hospitality), causing a boom time for the *Heurigen* and *Buschenschenken* at the expense of more serious wines. To some extent the attitudes which gave rise to the wine-scandal of 1985 were born of this time.

It would, however, be misleading to cast the pre-1985 period of Austrian winemaking in a wholly negative light. As has been amply proved by the many old wines sampled on my travels through the country, Austria never abandoned its dedication to excellence, and the rare bottle of pre-war wine which miraculously escaped the rapine of the Russian Army of occupation attests to the skill which went into winemaking in those days.

Klosterneuburg was at the forefront of viti-cultural experiment during those years when the innovative Dr Zweigelt was responsible for developing not only the excellent Zweigelt crossing of Blaufränkisch and St-Laurent but also the Blauburger crossed from Blaufränkisch and Blauer Portugieser. Pioneering work was also undertaken by Lenz Moser III in Rohrendorf-bei-Krems where the so-called 'high-culture' method of training vines was perfected.

The scandal that brought notoriety to Austrian wine in 1985 was a necessary evil. Without it it is doubtful whether the government and the growers would have begun to clean out the Augean stables and make an effort to take their rightful place among the galaxy of European stars. It would be hard to overestimate the shock the scandal caused among the more idealistic growers of the younger generation, and it still rankles today. Most of the bad blood disappeared when the law came down heavily on the perpetrators of the adulterations, and the men and women who came to the fore in their wake were fiercely determined to show outsiders that Austria was not just the butt of a few jokes about anti-freeze. The wines they have created are often very new, and in one or two cases the desire for novelty has led to an effusion of wrong-headedness. In the majority of cases, however, growers have remained aware of their best traditions – traditions which reach back more than two millennia through the checkered history of one of the youngest nations in Europe.

Steel vats in the 16th-century Sonnhof cellars in Langenlois.

CHAPTER II

The Wine Regions of Austria

*W*ine is made from fermented grapes and all grapes taste different. Suck on a ripe Cabernet Sauvignon berry or a ripe Pinot Noir and you will discern some of those flavours which so titillate the uninitiated reader of wine-speak. Geology is another factor in the taste of wine: when the yields are modest (which they should be) minerals in the soil contribute their five bob to the flavour of the wine. The final factor is the winemaker: fermentation and ageing techniques vary from cellar to cellar. Some winemakers, for example, like to flavour their wines with oak, this massively affects taste.

Austria possesses some of the most individual grape flavours in the world: nowhere else can claim the variety enshrined in Gruňer Veltliner, Zierfandler, Neuburger, Blaufränkisch, St-Laurent and Zweigelt; and that is not even mentioning grapes which prosper elsewhere, such as Rhine Riesling or Pinot Noir (Blauburgunder). Squashed between mountain ranges and the Pannonian plain, Austria has a geological multiplicity second to none: from slate and granite rock to gneiss, heavy loam, and loess. With the training that Austrian winemakers receive at Klosterneuburg or in Retz,

Autumn in a Lower Austrian vineyard.

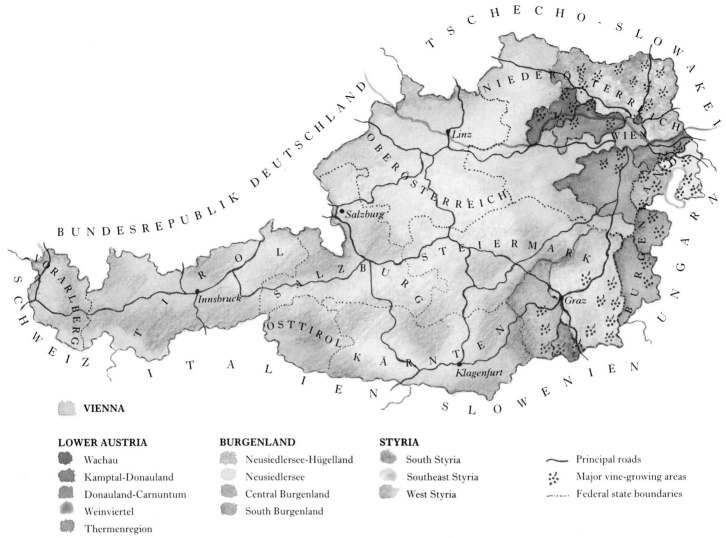

VIENNA

LOWER AUSTRIA	**BURGENLAND**	**STYRIA**	
Wachau	Neusiedlersee-Hügelland	South Styria	—— Principal roads
Kamptal-Donauland	Neusiedlersee	Southeast Styria	⁂ Major vine-growing areas
Donauland-Carnuntum	Central Burgenland	West Styria	······ Federal state boundaries
Weinviertel	South Burgenland		
Thermenregion			

(particularly in red-wine making), the technical standard can be very high indeed. These factors all contribute to Austria's position as one of the best (and least well-known) winemaking countries in the Old World.

Below I have listed some of the main grape varieties and their top producers. Naturally it is not exhaustive. Winemakers come and go and new stars, and indeed constellations, are constantly being discovered.

AUSTRIAN GRAPE VARIETIES

WHITE WINE GRAPES

Bouvier Synonyms: none. A grape developed by Clothar Bouvier in Lower Styria (now Slovenia) in the last century. It tends to be short in acidity and is chiefly used for high *Prädikat* wines. Best vinifiers: Kracher; Opitz.

Chardonnay Synonyms: Morillon; Feinburgunder. The first Chardonnay in Austria was probably the Morillon, planted in Styria in the last century. No one quite knows who was responsible for bringing it in from France and it was only identified as Chardonnay comparatively recently. Similarly, the grape was known as Feinburgunder in Vienna and Burgenland, until it was recognized as Chardonnay. One assumes that the grapes must have been brought in falsely labelled some 30 years ago.

Since that time the international Chardonnay craze has meant that few Austrian growers feel they can do without it.

Frühroter Veltliner

Grüner Veltliner

Best growers for the international wood-matured style: Bründlmayer; Gesellmann; Haus Marienberg; Malat-Bründlmayer; Mayer; Müller; Nittnaus; Reinisch; Schafler; Stiegelmar; Topf; Ernst Triebaumer; Wieninger.

Non-oaked style: Gesellmann; Gross (Morillon); Hiedler; Jamek; Kappel; Knoll; Neumayer; Polz; Sattler; Strell; Tement; Paul Triebaumer.

Sweet wines: Wenzel (*Ausbruch*).

Furmint No modern synonyms, but formerly called Zapfner, Zapfnete or Ordinäre. Both a green and a yellow variety exist. This is the grape which makes the great *Aszú* wines of Tokay in Hungary. In Austria only Robert Wenzel currently uses it, making both dry and sweet wines. About six other Rust growers have recently planted the yellow variety. Georg Stiegelmar in Gols has a little green Furmint which goes into his *gemischter Satz*. Best vinifier: Wenzel.

Frühroter Veltliner Synonym: Malvasier. Rather dull cousin of the Malvasia found in Italy and France, lacking the aromatic potential of the Southern European examples. Best producers: Feuerwehr-Wagner; Geyerhof; Leth.

Gewürztraminer Synonyms: Traminer, Roter Traminer, Gelber Traminer. The confused terminology stems from the fact that there are two strains of Gewürztraminer in Austria: a yellow and a red. In reality they are merely two clones of the same grape variety and have the same aromatic qualities. Austrian Gewürztraminer can be as good as any in the world. In Styria some producers make a rather stripped down style, which I feel is a waste of time, but elsewhere there is that haunting smell of yellow rose petals, gingerbread, spices and honey which exemplifies the best Gewürztraminer. The grape is best vinified dry at *Prädikat* level, although some producers make a convincing sweet wine. The best: Elfenhof; Ernst Triebaumer; Feuerwehr-Wagner; Haimer; Kracher; Lackner-Tinnacher; Leth; Mayer; Müller; Platzer; Prieler (schnapps); Stiegelmar; Stürgkh; Paul Triebaumer.

Goldburger No synonyms. Rather dull grape which sweetens well and makes *Prädikat* wines. Best growers: Haus Marienberg (*Eiswein*); Heinrich Salomon; Wachter (*Strohwein*).

Grüner Veltliner No modern synonyms but formerly called Weisser or Grüner Muskateller or Weissgipfler. It is by far the most widely planted variety accounting for 36 percent of Austria's vineyards. The Grüner Veltliner produces flavours which vary from smoky to lentils-and-white-pepper. When the grape is older than two or three years it develops slightly musty orangey notes. Most people prefer it when it is young and grapey. It is grown all over Austria, with the exception of Styria, but it is at its best in Lower Austria. It does not benefit from oak-ageing, but this has not prevented some growers from trying. Best growers: Aigner; Alzinger; Artner; Bründlmayer; Dinstlgut; Geyerhof; Glatzer; Haimer; Hiedler; Hirtzberger; Jamek; Jurtschitsch; Chorherrenstift Klosterneuburg; Kölbl; Knoll; Winzer Krems; Lagler; Leberwurst; Lehenhof; Leth; Malat-Bründlmayer;

Neuburger

Rhine Riesling

Mantlerhof; Messermayer; Metternisch'sche Weingüter; Lenz Moser; Neumayer; Neustifter; Nigl; Nikolaihof; Opitz; Osberger; Pichler; Pfaffl; Pitnauer (for his vermouth!); Pleil; Prager; Erich Salomon; Schmidl; Silberbichlerhof; Strell; Freie Weingärtner; Zull.

Müller-Thurgau Synonym: referred to as Riesling-Sylvaner throughout Austria. The Austrians are of course right (if pedantic), the Müller-Thurgau is a cross between the two grapes. Müller-Thurgau accounts for nine percent of Austria's vineyards; making it the second most widely planted vine. It is never particularly exciting but can be a useful jack-of-all-trades as it makes dry wines as well as *Prädikat* wines. At its most vulgar it has a catty character, which is called a *Sämlingston* in Austria (a reference to *Scheurebe*, called Sämling 88 here); but there are decent practitioners, especially in the Wachau. These are: Barmherzige Brüder (for brandy); Hirtzberger; Körper-Faulhammer; Landauer; Metternisch'sche Weingüter; Weinrieder.

Muskat-Ottonel The vulgar cousin of the Muskateller; this is sometimes referred to as the *Feinschmeckerter*. Useful in *Botrytis*-affected wines. Best growers: Kracher; Opitz; Osberger, Prieler (brandy).

Muskateller Synonyms: Gelber Muskateller, Muscat Lunel (Rust). A variety largely planted in the Wachau and South Styria but formerly popular in Rust. It produces Austria's noblest Muscat-style wines with real breed and character; these vary

from lemony to lemon-curdy, according to soil and the degree of residual sugar. Best producers: Jamek; Lackner-Tinnacher; Leth; Pichler; Platzer; Sattler; Wenzel.

Neuburger Synonyms: Grüner Burgunder (Wachau). As the synonym implies, the Austrians like to believe that this grape is a Burgundian or variety of the Pinot family. There is a story that the original cuttings were fished out of the Danube and no one can give a better reason for its existence than that. It is in fact one of Austria's most interesting grape varieties, producing beautifully textured dry wines with a pronounced nutty flavour. It also lends itself to late-picked styles which improve with bottle-age. Best producers: Alphart; Biegler; Geyerhof; Hirtzberger; Hofer; Winzer; Krems; Landauer; Nigl (aperitif wine); Nikolaihof; Paul Triebaumer; Schafler; Schandl; Wagentristl; Weinrieder.

Rhine Riesling Synonym: Weisser Riesling. The Rhine Riesling (to distinguish it from the Welschriesling) is one of Austria's great grapes. A Riesling from one of the best sites in the Wachau or Kamptal Donauland is easily a match for the highly prized wines of the Rhine and Mosel. With alcohol levels much higher than its German equivalents, the Austrian Riesling has a fullness of flavour comparable only with the very best of Alsace Rieslings. Young Wachau Rieslings tend to be steely and long on the palate; with time a limey flavour gives way to a honeyed taste, often accompanied by an aroma of petrol. The best wines are naturally more complex

Ruländer

Blauburgunder

still. Some surprisingly good Rieslings are occasionally encountered off the beaten track on primary rock soils; the most promising of these are in Styria. The best: Alzinger; Bründlmayer; Dolle; Freie Weingärtner; Hiedler; Hirtzberger; Jamek; Jurtschitsch; Kappel; Knoll; Lagler; Nigl; Nikolaihof; Osberger; Pichler; Polz; Prager; Erich Salomon; Schandl; Schmidl; Silberbichlerhof; Tement.

Roter Veltliner Synonym: Roter Muskateller. The cousin of the Grüner Veltliner is very rare these days. When well vinified it can produce quite exciting wines with rather musty, orangey notes and a good potential for ageing. In *Botrytis* years the Roter Veltliner generally performs better than the Grüner. One producer: the Mantlerhof.

Ruländer Synonyms: Pinot Gris, Grauburgunder, Grauer Mönch, Grauer Burgunder. One of the earliest grape varieties planted in Austria and one of the best. The Ruländer is chiefly planted in Burgenland and Styria, but there are good producers who plant elsewhere. The Ruländer lends itself to all styles of white wine from dry, unoaked whites to full, oaky styles and *Prädikat* wines. In general the word associated with the taste of Ruländer is "spice" combined with the aromas of flowers and sometimes root vegetables (radishes). As a *Prädikat* wine it is exemplary, producing rich, honeyed tones. Best producers: Bernreiter; Breyer; Bründlmayer, Elfenhof; Feiler-Artinger; Gross; Lackner-Tinnacher; Müller; Polz; Sattler; Schandl; Schröck; Silberbichlerhof.

Sauvignon Blanc Synonym: Muskat-Sylvaner.

Extremely fashionable grape variety which is currently taking Austria by storm. In Austria Sauvignon Blanc seems to be more valued for its pronounced acidity than for its aromatic qualities. When Austrian Sauvignon Blanc is good, however, it can be very good indeed with some fine grassy, smoky, artichoke or asparagus flavours. Most of the top wines come from Styria. Best producers: Ernst Triebaumer; Gross; Hirschmugl; Kollwentz; Leberl; Müller; Neumeister; Nittnaus; Polz; Sattler; Schilling; Stürgkh; Tement; Winkler-Hermaden.

Scheurebe Synonym: Sämling 88. White grape variety valued chiefly for its ability to rot nobly, but that must be the only noble thing in its nature; Scheurebe has an unfortunate ability to smell like urine, which the Austrians often excuse by a coy reference to a *Sämlingston*. When it is vinified well it can occasionally have an appealing aroma of grapefruit. Best producers: Gesellmann; Kracher; Leberl; Opitz.

Sylvaner Synonyms: Grüner Sylvaner. Rather angular and acidic grape variety which is little used in Austria. Best producers: Stadlmann; Topf.

Weissburgunder Synonyms: Weisser Burgunder, Klevner, Weisser Klevner, Pinot Blanc. A grape variety which arrived in Austria at the beginning of the last century, possibly from Moravia. The Weissburgunder makes some of Austria's finest whites. Nutty Weissburgunder wines may be obtained from virtually every region of Austria; only in the Wachau is it underrepresented. Best

Blauer Portugieser

Blauer Wildbacher

producers: Dolle; Feiler-Artinger; Glatzer; Gross; Heinrich; Hiedler; Jamek; Neumayer; Neustifter; Malat-Bründlmayer; Nikolaihof; Paul Triebaumer; Prieler; Reinisch; Sattler; Schilling; Stiegelmar; Taubenschuss; Topf.

Welschriesling Synonyms: Riesler. This is the Italian Riesling, the grape best known for making cheap Yugoslavian wines in Britain. The Welschriesling is highly fashionable in Austria where it is appreciated for its rapier-like acidity and its faint taste of apples or lemons. The Welschriesling is also an excellent grape at high *Prädikat* levels, as it rots nobly, producing fine *Ausbruch* and *Trockenbeerenauslese* wines. Best producers: Heinrich; Kracher (*Prädikat* wines); Landauer; Malat-Bründlmayer; Minkowitsch; Müller; Opitz; Platzer; Prieler; Paul Triebaumer (*Keltenwein*); Tement; Weinrieder (*Eiswein*).

Zierfandler and **Rotgipfler** Synonyms: Zierfandler is called Spätrot when blended with Rotgipfler. These two grapes are almost entirely confined to the northernmost villages of the Thermenregion; chiefly Gumpoldskirchen and Traiskirchen. One Austrian tried to convince me that the Zierfandler was in fact the same grape as the Californian Zinfandel, but I find this hard to believe, not least because the Zierfandler is a slightly pinky white grape and the Zinfandel is a hefty, tannic red! There is not much of either grape to be found: 127 hectares of Zierfandler and less than 30 hectares of Rotgipfler. They produce nicely structured wines which are best in the typical semi-

sweet *Gumpoldskirchner*, although some producers have attempted dry white and barrel-fermented styles. The Zierfandler is well structured and intense; the Rotgipfler has an intriguing aroma of brown bread and spiced peaches. Best producers: Biegler; Hofer; Kurz; Schellmann; Stadlmann; Weiss.

RED WINE GRAPES

Blauburger A cross between the Blaufränkisch and the Blauer Portugieser developed at Klosterneuburg in 1923 under the supervision of Dr Zweigelt. Blauburger can make some perfectly pleasant fruity red wines, but they rarely have any length. Best producers: Körper-Faulhammer; Lust; Opitz (*Eiswein*); WBS Retz.

Blauburgunder Synonyms: Blauer Burgunder, Pinot Noir, Blauer Spätburgunder. The Blauburgunder is easily the most successful of the up-and-coming red-wine varieties in Austria as it is quite capable of achieving levels of quality here which are comparable to the best outside Burgundy. Sadly, few Austrians seem to realise this and instead they cling foolhardily to the hope of achieving a fully ripe Cabernet Sauvignon in this coolish climate. Blauburgunder has been in Austria since the beginning of the last century, but it is only recently that growers have tried to make really serious wines with it. Best growers: Bründlmayer; Fischer; Gisperg; Grabner-Schierer (older vintages); Malat-Bründlmayer; Pasler-Bäck; Schandl; Sonnhof; Stiegelmar; Paul Triebaumer; WBS Retz.

Blaufränkisch

Zweigelt

Blauer Portugieser Synonym: Vöslauer. The grape which supplanted the Pinot Noir in the Thermenregion, Portugieser is a big, juicy grape with enormous yields. It can produce masses of rather boring red wine or, if properly controlled, a decent, if not overly long, fruity red. It is best known as the 'Vöslauer' of the spa towns of Baden and Bad Vöslau, but it grows elsewhere and may be adapted to different styles of wine. Best producers: Fischer; Gisperg; Grabner-Schierer; Lust; Reinisch (he makes a *solera* sherry from it!); WBS Retz; Wieninger.

Blauer Wildbacher No synonyms. The name is thought to come from the village of Wildbach near Deutschlandsberg. This is the *Schilcher* grape, making rosé wines with pronounced acidity and found only in Styria. Best producers: Koller; Lazarus; Müller.

Blaufränkisch No Austrian synonyms. One of Austria's most widely planted black grapes, it has often been confused with Gamay, but its origins are probably Hungarian rather than French. Blaufränkisch can make chunky raspberries and white-pepper scented wines but the grape has the drawback of being slightly short and fast-ageing. Some growers have successfully experimented with blending it with other varieties more calculated to make up for these defects. Best growers: Barmherzige Brüder; Feiler-Artinger; Gesellmann; Igler; Kopfensteiner; Krutzler; Leberl; Nittnaus; Schuster; Ernst Triebaumer; Paul Triebaumer.

Cabernet Sauvignon No synonyms in Austria. In Austria this is the nearest thing to the Holy Grail. Many pursue it, but it would be hard to say that anyone has so far possessed it. In a vintage such as the 1990, growers came nearest, producing musts with impressive levels of tannin and fruit to match. Best growers: Igler; Kollwentz; Leberl; Malat-Bründlmayer; Malteser Ritterorden; Nittnaus; Reinisch; Schandl; Wieninger.

St-Laurent No widely used synonyms. Austria's most tricky black grape; much given to disease at the time of the flowering. In Austria it is often said to be a member of the Pinot family and it certainly does seem similar to the Pinot Noir in its heady, sweet, strawberry aromas. It deserves to be more widely planted. Best growers: Fischer; Gisperg; Heinrich; Malat-Bründlmayer; Haus Marienberg; Nittnaus; Pitnauer; Platzer; Prieler; Reinisch; Schilling; Stiegelmar; Umathum.

Zweigelt Synonym: Rotburger. A grape developed by Dr Zweigelt at Klosterneuburg in 1922 by crossing the St-Laurent with the Blaufränkisch. Zweigelt can produce enormous crops if it is allowed to, but the best growers are those who rigorously thin their bunches to bring out all the cherry-flavoured fruitiness in the grape. Zweigelt has proved itself adaptable to most soils in Austria and has the advantage of providing the cooler regions of Lower Austria with a reliable red wine grape. Best producers: Alphart; Breyer; Fischer; Gisperg; Heinrich; Haus Marienberg; Iby; Kollwentz; Leberl; Lenz Moser; Müller; Pitnauer; Platzer; Strell; Umathum; Wagentristl.

VIENNA
(*WIEN*)

The Viennese are prone to boast that their city contains more hectares of vines than any other capital. Certainly it would be hard to imagine another so steeped in wine. Paris has vines in the Clos de Montmartre and the suburbs: these vines, however, are little more than municipal toys, and in 1980 the joke was that the administrators of the Suresnes vineyard were obliged to pin ripe bunches to the vines in order to prepare for the annual vintage festival. There was a Muscat vine in my London garden the last time I looked; but let's not quibble about things: Vienna has 720 hectares, which is about as many as can be found in the whole of England and Wales.

Of course, Vienna is not just a city, it is also a federal region, complete with its own parliament. During the Third Reich the city was enlarged to encompass not only Klosterneuburg to the west, but also the Südbahn to the south, with its vineyards around Gumpoldskirchen, Trais-kirchen, Baden and Bad Vöslau. After the war the

administrative area shrank and the city now contains fewer tracts of countryside; but it is on the semi-rural hills to the west that the lion's share of the vineyards is to be found.

Leaving aside those 19 vines in the Schwarzenbergplatz, the best tract of urban vines is the Alsegger vineyard in the 17th Bezirk, farmed by **Franz Mayer** of Heiligenstadt. Here trams rattle past the steep slope, noted for its steely Rieslings, which still belongs to the Benedictine monastery of Saint Peter in Salzburg. Six times a year, for one week only at a time, a local *Heurige* opens to dispense wines from the slope. During this period the cellars of the local vicarage are filled to bursting point.

There is an easier way to sample the wines of the Alsegger vineyard: you may purchase them from Franz Mayer's *Heurige* on the Pfarrplatz in Heiligenstadt; or better still from any one of Mayer's many importers around the world. Owning as many as 36 hectares, Mayer is the biggest man in

Viennese wine. His lively *Heurige* is open daily from February to December in a fine old building where, *he* maintains, Beethoven wrote part of his 9th Symphony. Musicologists have been known to snipe at this theory, but Heiligenstadt was a favourite retreat for the misanthropic composer, and virtually every path and brook retains some memory of his comings and goings.

Mayer now runs his business with two daughters and an Australian son-in-law called Mario Galler. Galler has a line in dirty jokes, which Mayer caps with amusing gobbets of Viennese vineyard lore. It was Mayer who told me of the five activities which preoccupy the Viennese grower during the winter months: racking wine; distilling schnapps; killing pigs; counting money; and making babies.

Mayer may be big, but size has not compromised quality. The *Heurige* business allows him to dis-

The Alsegger vineyard is one of the most urban of Vienna's surburban vineyards.

pose of 40 percent of his crop in the form of fresh, easy-drinking jug-wine; the other 60 percent is bottled and made to last. The proof of this was clear from Mayer's old wines from both the Alsegger vineyard and the Nussberg. From the Alsegger vineyard I have drunk a 1979 Rhine Riesling with all those rich, honey, blackcurrant and petrol aromas associated with the best wines of that grape. Mayer believes his wines from the Nussberg to be even better. Here he planted Chardonnay as long ago as 1976; but for me it is again the Rieslings which stand out, of which I tasted a splendid series going back to the 1970 vintage.

That Mayer should swear by the Nussberg should come as no surprise: the pedigree of this particular south-facing slope was established hundreds of years ago. Accompanied by another Viennese grower, **Martin Kierlinger** of Nussdorf, I climbed up to look at the vines one day in August 1991. For the most part they were trained high, according to the precepts of the Lenz Moser *Hochkultur* method; only here and there were a few clumps of vines still attached to their stakes, like the great Syrah vines which bristle on the hillsides of the northern Rhône Valley. Towards the crest of the hill are the vines of the Sekt company Kattus. True to their rather old-fashioned form, these Weissburgunder and Riesling vines have retained the earlier, low-culture training.

Kierlinger's best wines are also made from

Top left: Franz Mayer's Beethovenhaus Heurige.
Top right: Kattus' Jugendstil (art nouveau) labels.
Right: The Nussberg with Vienna in the background.

Weissburgunder and Rhine Riesling. Rieslings from the Nussberg have an intense lime and linden flowers aroma which marks them out as *Bergweine* (literally, wines from hillside sites). The Weissburgunders at their best have a faint smell of nuts. Kierlinger made some fine wines in the generally good 1990 vintage.

Feuerwehr-Wagner is another grower whose best wines come from those historic slopes of the Nussberg, Weidling and Klosterneuburg. The name itself derives from one Josef Wagner who was the last volunteer fireman in Heiligenstadt. As there were numerous Wagners in the village at the

time, Josef was distinguished by the name Fireman Wagner, and so it has stuck. A portrait of old Josef, complete with fireman's helmet, hangs in the main room of the *Heurige*: a pleasant jumble of historic rooms dating back to the sixteenth century, concealed behind a rather bland Biedermayer façade.

Today Andreas Feuerwehr-Wagner makes the wines. His 20-hectare vineyard is big by Viennese standards and he has a confusing array of grapes growing on his slopes. Some are museum pieces, such as the Braune Veltliner which he feeds into his traditional *Gemischten Satz* blend, along with Grüner Veltliner, Müller-Thurgau, Rhine Riesling, Chardonnay, Weissburgunder, Welschriesling, Gewürztraminer and Neuburger.

Not surprisingly, Rieslings come out top here. Feuerwehr-Wagner insists that Nussberg Rieslings should taste of nuts, which seems almost too good to be true; on the other hand there did seem to be a slight nuttiness about his 1990 Kabinett. Whatever nut aromas the 1979 Riesling Spätlese may have had, they had long since disappeared by the time I came to sample it; it had become a classic, petrolly old Riesling. A curiosity to look out for here is the Frühroter Veltliner or Malvasier wine from the Nussberg with its spicy, appley fruit. A little Gewürztraminer is also made from very old vines in Klosterneuburg.

Diametrically opposite the Nussberg and Kahlenberg, on the north bank of the Danube, is the Bisamberg. Fewer tourists visit the vineyards and *Heurigen* of this part of Vienna, but there are winemakers here who can make wines which are every bit as good.

The rising star of the Bisamberg is **Fritz Wieninger**, whose *Heurige* is in the rather unprepossessing suburb of Stammersdorf. Naturally, in order to win the approval of so many of Austria's wine writers, Wieninger has had to lead on the new varieties: Chardonnay and Cabernet Sauvignon. The Chardonnay is particularly successful; a 1989, aged in big tuns, had a good, lively acidity with some weighty mango/apricot fruit; a 1988 Kabinett Barrique from small Allier casks was noticeably fatter, with some good fruit-salad aromas. The Cabernet Sauvignon too is a fair stab at the style, although I felt that the 1989 needed a mite more complexity; something which might come from widening the palette of grapes involved. Wieninger makes a Beaujolais-style *nouveau* from Blauer Portugieser grapes with a smidgen of Zweigelt and a rather more serious Blauburger.

Herbert Schilling's *Heurige* is also in a rather charmless spot; although there is an airy garden which is occasionally visited by an energetic woodpecker. Schilling has patented a Wiener Augustin trademark for his wines; an allusion to the seventeenth-century buffoon, Augustin, who is commemorated in the song "O Du lieber Augustin" (from which the music of the British rugby song "Balls to Mr Bangelstein" was culled). 'Wiener Augustin' labels are now used for all Schilling's top wines, ie those sold in Bordeaux bottles.

One of Schilling's most successful wines is his Sauvignon Blanc, which is virtually reserved for the restaurant Steinerne Eule in Vienna's 7th Bezirk. Only 800 litres of this grassy, peachy wine are made, so it might merit a special trip to the restaurant. The Weissburgunder is made in some-thing like commercial quantities and is possibly Schilling's best white with its orange and nut character; although they are occasionally pipped at the post by his Rieslings. Of the latter, the 1988 was extremely good. Schilling also makes a good red from his St-Laurent vines; the 1990 here was his personal best with its rich, deep, plummy fruit. A 1985 was still on top form when I tasted it in 1991.

Gertrude Bernreiter's *Heurige* is in neighbouring Jedlersdorf while all of her 9.5 hectares are on the Bisamberg. These days Frau Bernreiter takes care of feeding visitors to the *Heurige* (which includes some of Austria's leading political personalities), and it is her son Peter who looks after the winemaking.

Since he took over, **Peter Bernreiter** has had considerable success with his wines at Austrian shows. His Weissburgunders have been best received with the lovely 1989 making its way into the Salon for the 200 best Austrian wines of the year. The 1988 was nominated for the title of

Above: Feuerwehr-Wagner: the Biedermayer façade of the Heurige *at vintage time.*
Right: The Bisamberg vineyard on the northern side of the Danube.

Austrian Federal Champion in its class; it is a rather truffly, meaty wine and I personally far preferred the 1989 which, with its intense incense character, would make a fine accompaniment to foie gras. Bernreiter makes a little Grüner Veltliner, but sighs *"I' find' der Veltliner ist nicht die optimale Sorte für'n Bisamberg"*, (I don't think it's the best cultivar for the Bisamberg).

In my opinion Bernreiter's star wine is his Ruländer. In most years his vines are able to produce wines at *Spätlese* or *Auslese* level on the sandy loam soils of the hill. The 1990 Auslese has a small amount of residual sugar behind the peach and lychee fruit; the 1988 Spätlese is classic stuff, with its full peach and mandarin character; the 1986 Spätlese shows signs of having been visited by a small amount of *Botrytis*.

The situation on the Bisamberg hill is no different from that on the hills south of the Danube: the vast majority of the vines of Vienna are in the hands of amateur winemakers who have little or no care about the quality of wines they produce. Peter Bernreiter estimates that only one fifth of the Bisamberg is put to good use, but if one were to compile a hit-list of the best winemakers in Vienna, Leopold Breyer would certainly come top, or pretty near the top. Breyer also has a (rather lacklustre) *Heurige* in Jedlersdorf, as well as a pretty old cellar in the *Kellergasse* (cellar lane) which climbs the steep slopes of the Bisamberg, where the main part of his vineyards are to be found. A small plot in next-door Gerasdorf is used only for *Schankwein*; that is, wine for the *Heurige*.

Leopold Breyer is a former car-mechanic turned winemaker and occasional poet who writes in Viennese dialect about the hardships of his *métier*. Breyer's Rhine Rieslings prove that in a good year the Bisamberg can make Riesling wines with as much breed as those from the Nussberg or the Kahlenberg. The 1990 seemed to be dominated by enchanting white-chocolate and Turkish-delight flavours in its youth, while both the 1989 and the 1987 were exemplary Rieslings of the plumper style. The very best to date is the black-currant-dominated 1986.

Breyer makes a good Ruländer, of which the dry Auslese of the 1986 vintage is the best example I have tasted. Unlike most of the other growers in Vienna, Breyer actually specialises in reds, producing a fine *cuvée* from Zweigelt and Blauer Portugieser, as well as an award-winning straight Zweigelt wine. These red wines Breyer houses in barrels of Manhartsberger oak from the Kamptal region. Manhartsberger appears to be a white oak similar to those used in Kentucky for adding flavour to Bourbon whiskey, and some people might find its flavours a little too domineering for a delicate wine. To Breyer's Zweigelt/Portugieser blend it adds a heavy vanilla-sugar flavour and a spicy character associated with Bourbon. The straight Zweigelt is his best red, with its pronounced chocolate/cherry character. The 1986 vintage had the honour of winning an Oscar at VinExpo in Bordeaux; it is one of the fullest representations of the Zweigelt I have tasted and a remarkable success with its nutty, blackberry fruit.

LOWER AUSTRIA
(NIEDERÖSTERREICH)

Retz

Pulkau

Haugsdorf

Falkenstein

Poysbrunn

Mailberg

Poysdorf

Eggenburg

Röschitz

V

Wilfersdorf

Maissau

Hollabrunn

I

Hobersbrunn

E

Zöbing

Longenlois

Strass

Senftenberg

Hadersdorf

Kirchberg am Wagram

R

Mannersdorf

Weissenkirchen

Krems

Gedersdorf

Wolkersdorf

Dürnstein

Joching

Rohrendorf

Wösendorf

Furth Palt

D O N A U

Spitz

Mautern

Göttweig

Tulln

Klosterneuburg

T

DONAULAND-CARNUNTUM

E

W A C H A U

WIEN

L

D O N A U

Petronell-Carnuntu

Percholdsdorf

Mödling

DONAULAND - CARNUNTUM

Göttlesbrunn

Höflein

Gumpoldskirchen

Guntramsdorf

Bruck an der Leitha

Baden

Traiskirchen

Sooss

Bad Vöslau

Steinfelden

Tattendorf

T H E R M E N R E G I O N

Major vine-growing areas

Wine routes

① K A M P T A L - D O N A U L A N D

WACHAU

The Danube in the Wachau above Krems.

The first thing which strikes all but the most culturally jaundiced visitors to the Wachau is the sublimity of the scenery. Few, if any, parts of the wine-lover's world can match it for beauty; possibly only one, the Douro Valley in Portugal. After the magnificent monastery of Melk, the Danube flows past Spitz then sweeps down to a tight S-bend just before Krems. On either side of the waterway rise great peaks terraced with vines. At their feet lie some of the loveliest towns and villages in Lower Austria: Unterloiben, Weissenkirchen, Joching, Wösendorf, St-Michael, Spitz, Mautern and of course, Dürnstein. And in the heart of Dürnstein are the blue-painted monastery and *Schloss*, clustered below the ruined fortress where, eight centuries ago, an Austrian ruler incarcerated the English King, Richard the Lionheart.

If those visitors stop at any one of the many good restaurants which line the banks of the Danube they will discover that other great asset of the Wachau: the wines. The Wachau is without a shadow of a doubt Austria's greatest region for dry white wines. Here is a concentration of great vineyards such as exists nowhere else in the country, producing wines with immense 'breed'. The best of these are Rhine Rieslings for the Wachau is one of the world's great Riesling areas while on the flatter land nearer the river are some of the country's quintessential Grüner Veltliners.

The good restaurants are the third attraction of the Wachau. Almost as soon as you pass the last great vineyard in Stein (the Steiner Hund), you fall on the villages of Unterloiben and Oberloiben. Here. Loibnerhof is owned by the Knoll family, and as luck would have it **Emmerich Knoll** is one of the Wachau's most talented winemakers. So the way to experience Loibnerhof is to ask the waitress to serve different wines with each course.

This is precisely what I did when I was there on a cold February day. With an aspic of sucking pig came a Grüner Veltliner Steinfeder 1989 from Ried Schütt. *Steinfeder* is the lightest of the Wachau categories, invented in 1985 by the Vinea Wachau association in the wake of the wine scandal. The

45

idea was to promote only the dry white wines of the region, giving them distinctive names which would apply only to the Wachau. *Steinfeder* wines must be natural and unchaptalised, with a maximum alcoholic degree of 10.7. The next category up is the *Federspiel*; the same rules about chaptalisation apply but these dry wines may go up to 11.9°. The final category for dry, unchaptalised Wachau whites is *Smaragd* (named after the emerald-green Idex lizard found locally). These are the best and must achieve a must weight of at least 90° *Oechsle*.

Back to the Schütt Steinfeder 1989: it had a classically angular Wachau fruitiness with a slight redolence of rhubarb. To accompany some wild boar ham came another Veltliner from the 1989 vintage, this time a *Federspiel* with rather more of the pepper associated with the grape. The *Smaragd* wine from the Loibenberg came with a Veltliner soup (*see p 130*). It was still a little closed with some pear-aniseed character.

The first Rhine Riesling accompanied a collection of *Tascherl* (rather like large ravioli) filled with spinach, lamb fillet and *Grammeln*. It was a Steiner Pfaffenberg 1989 with a racy, limey character and beautiful length. Then came Danube catfish, or *Wels*, with a 1988 Chardonnay Smaragd with a pronounced structure, not at all the fat sort of international-style Chardonnay. A second wine was presented with this dish: a Riesling Smaragd 1989 from the Ried Schütt with a tight Riesling structure which should mean it ages divinely. Finally, with a copious selection of desserts came a 1986 Riesling Spätlese from Schütt (the Wachau classifications do not apply to wines with residual sugar). Again a classy wine destined for a long life, but with insufficient sweetness to handle the poppy-seed *Nudeln*; better for this was a Loibner Grüner Veltliner Beerenauslese 1983.

The **Winzergenossenschaft Dinstlgut Loiben** shares some of these top sites with Emmerich Knoll, notably Schütt and the Loibenberg. The Dinstlgut is a cooperative vinifying the grapes of 740 members, but only 40 percent of these are actually in the Wachau. Before my tasting at the Dinstlgut, the oenologist drove me up to the top of the Loibenberg to point out the best vineyard sites at the eastern end of the region. It was a stunning view, almost reminiscent of the top of the hill at

Hermitage in the Rhône, with the granite cliffs of Tournon rising up on the west bank of the river. There at the bottom, on the gneiss soils, were the main vineyards for Grüner Veltliner (still the main variety here, Riesling accounts for a mere eight percent). He then directed my attention to the Riesling vineyards on the steep sites with their granite bedrock; all except one, that is, for the Loibner Burgstall is actually on sandy loam.

As well as vinifying the grapes of their many members, the Dinstlgut Loiben also makes the wines of the well-known **Baron Geymüller** estate in Kamptal-Donauland. The 1990 Grüner Veltliner from Geymüller proved a promising introduction to our tasting that day: it was from the Ried Schifer with a big, deep bouquet of honey from its very low-yielding vines. Another Veltliner 1990 from Schütt in the Wachau proved rather fatter. At the eastern end of the Wachau the wines are

'broader', as a result of a greater Pannonian influence which reportedly follows the route of the Danube. It was interesting to try some older Veltliners from Schütt, such as a 1979 with a bouquet of toast and pea-soup with a hint of incense; the 1975 had turned golden, throwing off a nose reminiscent of a ripe Neuburger to reveal oranges, caramel and walnuts.

Our Rieslings kicked off with another Geymüller 1990, this time from the Ried Goldberg with a delightful structure and racy Riesling aromas. The 1990s at the Dinstlgut were generally more successful than the 1989s, with good wines from the Burgstall and from Schütt. The cooperative still retains some stunning old wines which they sell for modest prices; one which I particularly admired was a dry Riesling from the 1981 vintage with some really authentic petrol, toast and lime aromas.

Leo Alzinger is one of the darlings of the Austrian wine press; a rare achievement perhaps for a man without Cabernet Sauvignon, but he does admit to having a little Chardonnay, even if he is reluctant to bring it out. His 4.4-hectare estate occupies some of the best sites in Loiben and is planted for the main with Grüner Veltliner and Rhine Riesling.

Sadly, my arrival at Alzinger's house occurred only a few hours after the departure of the Danube. The river burst its banks in the summer of 1991, causing severe damage to property in the lower lying villages. Understandably, Alzinger had other things on his mind than my visit, but we did have a chance to look at some of his 1990s: a Grüner Veltliner Steinfeder with a marked white-pepper-and-lentils character; a Federspiel from the Hochstrasser vineyard with an impressive structure and a Smaragd from different sites with some classic lentil and pear aromas. His Rieslings were made with the same care. I tried two Smaragds: one from the Loibenberg and another from the Höhereck. Both had 13°; both were superb with that seemingly endless length which marks out great Riesling.

Franz Xaver Pichler's house and cellars are only a few kilometres away in Oberloiben. His estate is much the same size as Alzinger's and his wines enjoy (if that is possible) even greater esteem among the Austrian wine-loving public. Franz Xaver took over from his father in 1971 and since 1983 he has made only *Qualitätsweine* and has abandoned chaptalisation. Pichler is a slightly shy man and, as is so often the case, his wines seem to echo his reserve. 1990 was obviously a wonderful year for him; his Veltliners, such as the *Smaragds* from the Loibner Berg and Von den Terrassen, were a notable success. Rieslings too showed the same mastery with four *Smaragd* wines, one of which, the Oberhauser, was picked as late as 6 November. The best of the four was probably the Dürnsteiner Kellerberg with its lime/lemon fruit.

Wines as compact as these age beautifully – even the Grüner Veltliners, as was demonstrated by a superb Honifogl 1986. (*Honifogl* was the first incarnation of *Smaragd*, but the name had to be abandoned when a lady owning a few vines in Langenlois complained, claiming it compromised her

Grüner Veltliner vines below the mediaeval walls of Dürnstein.

An old town house in a picturesque corner of Dürnstein.

sales. Her name was Frau Honifogl.) A 1986 Riesling from the Dürnsteiner Kellerberg was beautifully long and rich in honey aromas. These notes were even stronger in a 1975 Riesling from the Loibnerberg in which a maltiness had crept in. Pichler makes a couple of other wines of note: a Gelber Muskateller with an attractive lemon-balm bouquet and a Sauvignon Blanc. Pichler is very happy with his Sauvignon, but I did not find anything typical in the 1990 I tried.

The **Freie Weingärtner Wachau** cooperative occupies the site of a large former monastery which was closed down by Leopold II in 1790. The Emperor granted the land to the Starhemberg family, aristocrats who had particularly distinguished themselves repelling the Turks a century before. It was still in their hands in 1938 when Prince Ernst Rüdiger von Starhemberg had to flee to avoid a severe contretemps with Austria's new rulers. Hitler's men granted the Starhemberg lands to the local growers who started the cooperative that year. After 1945 they had to make pecuniary amends to the Prince in order to hang on to it.

The Freie Weingärtner is in some ways a model cooperative. There is no question of compromising quality, and year after year they produce some of the best wines in the Wachau. There were some exemplary Grüner Veltliners in 1986 and 1988, and I even tasted a hugely fruity 1977 Spätlese, which is still for sale. The Rieslings are naturally the best here, especially those from the Ried Achleiten in Weissenkirchen. The 1988, with its elegant structure, showed the site at its best. The 1986 Achlei-

ten, which I drank in the Florianihof in Weissenkirchen, was full of that limes and petrol character I love in Riesling.

Together with Josef Jamek in Joching, old **Franz Prager** in Weissenkirchen was the pioneer of dry white wines in the Wachau. These two men saw that the right path was to move away from the *lieblich* semi-sweet wines and move towards the angular, structured style so much appreciated by wine lovers in Austria and Germany today. Prager has now taken the back seat and the motive force in the estate today is provided by his son-in-law, Anton Bodenstein.

Prager has some impressive Grüner Veltliners as proof that he takes the grape seriously: a 1990 Steinfeder from Ried Steinriegl had an interesting lemon barley-water taste; while a 1990 Federspiel from Ried Hinter der Burg was rather smoky; a Smaragd from 50-year-old vines in Steinriegl was predictably intense. Some of the Prager Rieslings come from the Ried Ritzling, which *they* say is the *fons et origo* of the Riesling grape. Much as I like this story, I do not believe it: Riesling is only a very recent arrival to Wachau and more ancient reports suggest that the "sour Wachauer" was not made of the best-quality cultivars.

The Prager Rieslings must be a great improvement on those much-derided Wachau wines of times past; although, of all I have tasted, I have to say that the 1990 from the Ried Ritzling was the one that impressed me least. Of the 1990s I far preferred the *Federspiel* and the *Smaragd* from Steinriegl as well as the *Smaragd* from Ried Achleiten. In the case of the latter the fermentation refused to budge at 7.5g/l residual sugar, leaving the wine with a flavour of sweet, ripe pears. In 1990 Prager made an Auslese in the Ried Klaus, something which happens only once in a decade. Only 900 litres were made of this lovely, lime-scented wine. A 1986 from the same vineyard had this character too, along with a hint of lemon-peel and blackcurrants.

That other Wachau pioneer, **Josef Jamek**, shares some of the same vineyards. He is based in Joching, only a few kilometres up the road. Jamek is in his mid-70s now, a powerfully built man who can still lift doors off their hinges with apparent ease. Even by the 1950s Jamek had plotted his course: he was going to make dry wines with less alcohol. Later he took the decision to perform a malolactic fermentation on his whites, realising that this would allow him to lower sulphur levels. As far as the Wachau is concerned he is virtually alone in this. Recently there have been worries about his succession: Jamek has four daughters and it is hoped that one of these will carry on the good work in Joching.

Jamek also runs a restaurant of that name, one of the best in the region, and it is recommended that visitors try out his excellent wines by the glass with a meal there. I did this, sampling a sappy Grüner Veltliner Marienfeld 1990 with a *Saumaise* (a round smoked-pork sausage). With some lamb-ham and an aspic of chanterelles came a wine from one of Jamek's most famous sites: the Ried Klaus. This was a 1990 Riesling Federspiel with classic, limey fruit. With a guinea-fowl stuffed with chicken livers on a bed of cabbage came a 1990 Federspiel Chardonnay from the Zweikreuzgarten. This was an angular Chardonnay without oak. Later the waitress brought another 1990, this time a Weissburgunder Hochrain Federspiel; it was faintly spritzig with a nutty, cabbagey character which I did not much like. Lastly, with an elderflower sorbet, came a 1989 Gelber Muskateller from the Ried Kollmitz with a pretty, yellow rose character.

Karl Lagler and his family have a house and *Buschenschank* in Spitz. I know his wines less well than some in the Wachau as my visit occurred at a time when he, like Leo Alzinger, was busy fighting back the waters of the Danube from his vineyards beside the river. Later I was told he was in the shower, and might well be still there for he had not re-emerged by the time I left. Lagler's best *Ried* is Steinborz on which he grows both Grüner Veltliner and Riesling. Elsewhere he has quite a lot of Müller-Thurgau and Neuburger which is sometimes blended with Weissburgunder. The 1990 Grüner Veltliner Steinfeder from Hochrain was good and lentilly; the Federspiel from Burgberg rather fruitier. The best 1990 was the Smaragd from Steinborz, grown on granite and gneiss with its plump, lentil taste. A Riesling Smaragd 1990 from the same vineyard was wonderfully intense.

Lagler's neighbour, **Franz Hirtzberger**, was

The Hirtzberger vineyards in Spitz. A view from the Honivogl to the Tausendeimerberg with the Danube in the background.

also absent in the vineyards; but his wife was kind enough to take me there before his return to look at the ripening grapes. This was more self-sacrificial than I had anticipated: hearing a very Catholic expletive of "*Maria und Josef!*", I turned round to find that she had snapped off one of her high heels on the steep slope of the Singerriedel. We then ran into Herr Hirtzberger senior who waved at the rocky soil with a magisterial sweep and sighed "*Ach! Sehen sie, ich bin ein steinreicher Mann!*" (As you can see I'm rich in stones. In German *steinreich* also means as rich as Croesus). A few moments later the genial Franz arrived and continued the tour of his very traditional cellars.

It was in the sixteenth-century courtyard house that we tasted some of the best wines in the Wachau (and also in Austria). Franz Hirtzberger was one of the leading lights in the creation of the distinctive Wachau quality gradations in 1985. The ill-fated Honifogl was one of his own vineyards: a Grüner Veltliner *Ried* which always attained 13° of alcohol even in poor years. He has other Veltliners besides this: from the Donaugarten, or riverside vineyard, came the 1990 Steinfeder with the lightest fruit; a Federspiel, came from the Rotes Tor with its granite soils. In 1990 he also harvested a Smaragd here with peachy, apricoty notes. The Smaragd was the densest of the Honifogl wines; I do not know if this was autosuggestion, but I found strong honey flavours.

The Rieslings were the best of all. In the 1990 vintage there was a Federspiel Hochrain with a creamy lime and bay-leaf taste and a Hochrain Smaragd with superb length behind a rather more muted nose. The best Riesling came from the Singerriedel, where the Smaragd had a minerally, limey quality: a wine to keep for years and years. We finished off with some older wines: a 1983 Spätlese from Hochrain (before *Smaragd* became the accepted term) with rich honey, lime and petrol aromas; and another Hochrain Spätlese, this time a 1975. This one was marked by perfectly mature, rose-petal notes.

A chunk of the Wachau is on the south side of the river, around the old Roman city of Mautern. **Friedrich Hutter's** Silberbichlerhof estate is a little way to the south of the town. Two thirds of his eight hectares are beside the house, the other third

is on the slopes of Loiben. Three quarters of his wines are Veltliner and he has a tiny amount of St-Laurent. Recently he has replanted some Ruländer of which he thinks highly. His best Grüner Veltliner comes from the Rothenhof vineyard in Loiben; a 1990 Smaragd was impressive. The Mautern Rieslings have a nice little scent of honey, as in the 1990 Steinfeder from the Silberbichl. The wines from the Loibenberg are rich in apricot flavours. Look out too for some of Hutter's older Ruländers.

The best estate in Mautern, indeed the best on the south bank of the river, is the Nikolaihof owned by **Nikolaus Saahs** and his wife. The Nikolaihof itself is one of the most enchanting buildings I know. You could teach European civilisation here, giving a different lesson in each room: there is a Roman room, a Romanesque room, a vaulted Gothic chapel, a Baroque suite, a Biedermeyer

Left: One of Austria's most famous vineyards, the Steiner Hund, in the February snow.
Below: The mediaeval chapel in the courtyard of the Nikolaihof estate in Krems.

suite and in the leafy courtyard, where the Saahs' children are in evidence pitting apricots for *Marillenschnaps*, is a linden planted to commemorate Emperor Franz Josef's 60th jubilee.

In such a delightful house one hopes·that the wines will match up to the architecture: they do, in fact they are better structured on the whole. Like the Silberbichlerhof, the Saahs family have vines on both sides of the river, including a small part of the famous Steiner Hund. As much as 45 percent of their vines are steely Rieslings; the rest is Veltliner, besides a little amount of Neuburger, Frühroter Veltliner and Weissburgunder.

The Nikolaihof's best Grüner Veltliner vineyard is Im Weingebirge. It is based on granitic soil which produces Veltliners one might confuse with Rieslings. A 1986 Honifogl had developed some old Veltliner character: toast and oranges. There are good Neuburgers here too with big, fat, peachy fruit; Saahs rather eccentrically calls them Grüner Burgunders. A 1990 Weissburgunder Smaragd Baumgarten was destined for a long innings and both the Neuburger and the Weissburgunder join Riesling and Grüner Veltliner in the idiosyncratic Cuvée Elisabeth with its smoky, nutty fruit. Elisabeth is the name of their eldest daughter.

Of course, the best Nikolaihof wines are the Rieslings. Once again 1990 proved a superlative year, better than any since 1986. The Federspiel Vom Stein is precisely what Saahs is aiming for with its tight, elegant structure; the Smaragd of the same year and same vineyard was obviously a shade fuller but also a mite more closed a year after the harvest. It will be worth waiting for; certainly the 1977 Steiner Hund Riesling bore this out, this old *Spätlese* had matured into a creamy, nutty concoction, with some hints not only of violets but also Seville oranges.

KAMPTAL-DONAULAND

With Kamptal-Donauland we come to a region which contains some of Austria's most elegant and aristocratic wines. Some, because once again the region, created in 1985, lacks coherence and is best divided into four: Kaiserstiege around Rohrendorf, notable for the large number of Mosers who live and work in the vicinity; the hills to the south of the Danube which surround the Benedictine monastery of Göttweig; the valley of the Kamp river; and finally the valley of the Krems river.

Together with Melk and Klosterneuburg, Göttweig is one of Austria's most impressive religious houses. The baroque monastery sits magnificently on top of its hill, staring out towards the wine towns of Krems and Langenlois. The **Benedictine monks** still possess a 30-hectare vineyard and much of its wine is sold through their monastic tavern near the Hofburg Palace in Vienna. They are not, however, among Austria's best-known wines.

The same could not be said of the production of **Gerald Malat** in Furth-Palt just below Göttweig. Malat-Bründlmayer (Malat married the sister of Willi Bründlmayer of Langenlois and appended her name to his own on his labels) is one of Austria's most fashionable producers. Malat has around 20 hectares from which he produces wine with virtually every form of technical wizardry imaginable. The squeaky-clean cellars dazzle with steel and new oak from Demtos or Séguin Moreau. Malat demonstrates the workings of this wine laboratory with unconcealed pride; a big, bluff Falstaffian character exuding confidence.

Wines are tasted in a flashy poligonal office filled with modern art. Each wine gets an 'art label', bottles come from Italy and clones are rigourously imported from wherever Malat feels the grape is at its best: Ruländer from Italy, Weissburgunder from France, Cabernet Sauvignon from Bordeaux. It would be hard to list all the good wines which emerge from Malat's cellars. One thing which can safely be said of him is that he is reliable, even the simplest Welschriesling or Grüner Veltliner is bound to be good. The Weissburgunder is kept on its lees in cask to give it a distinctive character; the

A view of Mautern in the Danube from the Steiner Hund.

steely Rhine Riesling is grown on primary rock; the Ruländer has an endearing spiciness. Of all his whites one gets the impression that Malat is fondest of his Chardonnay, 40 percent of which is fermented in new oak (the rest in steel). The oak is still dominant in the 1990 but it is good Chardonnay; one of Austria's best attempts at this international idiom.

Certainly one of Malat's best reds is the seemingly incense-laden St-Laurent, but he himself is more interested in his Cabernet Sauvignon; indeed, he is almost obsessed with this wine. I found the 1988 slightly too herbaceous for my liking, but the 1990 must be just about the best Cabernet made in Austria to date. In my opinion his 1988 Blauburgunder is even more promising with its authentically earthy style.

Also in Furth is the Geyerhof where **Ilse Maier** now makes the wine on the family estate. The Maiers live in a modern house smack opposite the sadly dilapidated old *Herrenhaus* (the equivalent of a manor house) which gives its name to the estate. Frau Maier's wines are all organic now. Grüner Veltliner is the main variety here and by centrifuging the wine she manages to do without sulphur dioxide. The best Veltliner comes from the Hoher Rain vineyard. Frau Maier also makes a pretty Frühroter Veltliner and Neuburger as well as an interesting red wine made from a blend of Blauburger, Blauer Portugieser and ten percent Cabernet Sauvignon. When I visited her in August she was preparing to make her *Marillenbrand* (Apricot schnapps); fermenting ripe fruit in huge plastic containers. Frau Maier also makes a pleasant *Zwetschkenbrand* (plum schnapps) as well as fruit schnapps from Müller-Thurgau and Cabernet Sauvignon grapes.

Wolfgang Aigner is across the river from Furth in the lovely old town of Krems. Aigner is fairly typical of the thrusting new generation of Austrian growers: both his father and grandfather used to take their grapes to the cooperative, but Aigner has decided to make the wine himself and with considerable success. His gooseberry and pineapple-scented 1989 Grüner Veltliner was judged the best Veltliner of the year in that vintage, and his 1990s from Kremser Sandgrube and Kremser Weinzierlberg are just as good, if not better.

Karl Ditz's Lehenhof shares some of those top sites with Aigner, and he also possesses a lovely old cellar on the Weinzierlberg itself. The estate's history can be traced back some 800 years. Ditz also specialises in Grüner Veltliner from the Weinzierlberg, of which I remember an excellent 1989 (the 1990 seemed to lack acidity). He also has other good things like his Bergweine Rhine Rieslings from Kremsleiten, of which the 1990 elicited "lime, almond, acacia honey" when I tasted it the August following the vintage. The 1988 was already developing a classic petrol aroma. Look out also for his Neuburgers with their creamy, nutty fruit. Ditz occasionally makes a *Prädikat* wine from this grape: an *Eiswein* or, in an Indian summer like 1981, a wonderfully intense *Trockenbeerenauslese*. Ditz also makes a good Chardonnay which goes into large wood but does not get the new-oak-barrel treatment.

Had they so chosen, both Aigner and Ditz could have taken their grapes to the cooperative cellar, the **Winzer Krems**, and exchanged them for cash. The Winzer Krems work to a system of rewards and punishments so that a kilo of grapes can fetch anything from 2 to 20 Schillings. Besides making the wines of its *coopérateurs*, Winzer Krems also vinify the grapes of **Graf Bubna** in Donauland-Carnuntum, making quite earthy Grüner Veltliners. Their best Kremser Veltliners are from the Ried Goldberg. Also impressive was a 1990 Rhine Riesling from Kremser Kremsleiten and a lovely walnut-tasting 1990 Neuburger from the Strasser Gaisberg vineyard.

The town of Krems spills out along the Danube, eventually becoming the town of Stein at the gates of the Wachau. Between Krems and Stein is Und: not the connecting word you might think but a corruption of Hundis or Hunding, who was once lord of these parts. In Und is the Kloster Und vinothèque where visitors can taste a very wide range of the best wines of Austria in a converted monastery. **Erich Salomon** created the vinothèque and also owns the nearby Undhof, another former monastery which was dissolved by the reforming Emperor Leopold II in 1792.

The Undhof and Salomon are responsible for some of the very best Grüner Veltliners and Rhine Rieslings in Austria. Most of the Veltliner comes from a three-hectare plot directly behind the house, hemmed in on all sides by urban sprawl. The worst element of this urbanism is the high security prison; from the vineyard one is aware of 1,000 pairs of captive eyes coveting your liberty. The *Ried* is not called Gefängnisberg (prison-hill), however, but Wieden and it makes classic Veltliner, often marked by a little whiff of cloves. Salomon's best Riesling land is on the amphitheatre of steep hills which looks down on Stein and Und: they are the Ried Kögl, Steiner Pfaffenberg and Steiner Hund. *À propos* of the last *Ried*, some Austrians will have you believe that it acquired its name when the owner of the vineyard sold it in exchange for an edible dog. This is not true; the Steiner Hund's name comes from the same origin as Und the town.

The Steiner Hund is one of the most famous vineyards in Austria, producing Rieslings of great intensity of character which fully match anything from the Rhine or the Mosel. The wines seem to have a nuttiness to them; a slight aroma of walnuts which marks them out. The next-door Pfaffenberg is owned by a monastery in Passau, Bavaria and the monks rent the vines to Salomon. The 1989 was rather more pineappley in character. Salomon's largest Riesling vineyard is Kögl, which produces an intensely flavoursome Riesling which appears to last for ever. I have enjoyed a 1966 Kögl which was a beautiful old wine; and better still a 1932! This incredibly rare treat was saved from the ravaging Russian squaddies by Salomon's father who wisely concealed his best wine in an empty cask. The Ivans tapped at the wood but hearing only a hollow resonance they passed on by.

Krems is not just the name of a town, it is also a river and the valley of the river produces some exceptional wines too. The best of these are made by **Josef Nigl** in Senftenberg. It is not for nothing that I first met one of Austria's best-known wine personalities, Father Johann Denk, around the Nigl kitchen table. Denk is a priest in the nearby Waldviertel who is much in demand for his fine palate; to find Denk perched over a glass is a very good omen.

Nigl's wines were stunning; from a series of green lentil- or haricot bean-scented Grüner Veltliners (Father Denk found the fragrance of cornflowers) grown in the primary rock soils of Ried

Left: Vineyards in Kamptal Donauland.
Below: Attaching young vines to stakes in the Kamptal.

Pellingen to the quite magnificent Rhine Rieslings from the stony ground of Ried Rammeln, Hochäcker or Kremsleiten. The 1990s have wonderful breed while there are still tremendous wines from the 1988, 1986 and 1985 vintages. Father Denk was clearly enjoying himself that evening every bit as much as I – he kept exclaiming "*Super Floschen!*" (wonderful bottles) after each wine. I left after the last wine, a Neuburger made as an aperitif wine which I thought would go very well with eggs; "*Probier ma!*" (let's see), chortled Denk who dived with both hands into a dish of egg mayonnaise, clearly delighted with the excuse to try out my theory.

Strass im Strassertale is in the Kamptal. This village owes its fame largely to the Heiligenstein vineyard which produces wines (above all Grüner Veltliners and Rhine Rieslings) of great breed and finesse. The biggest producer here is **Helmut Osberger** who, besides his own 50 hectares of vineyards and orchards, buys in grapes from local producers for some of his cheaper brands. Osberger's activities as a *négociant-éléveur* are somewhat out of key with the Austrian wine world as it has existed since the dark days of the scandal.

Osberger himself complains that his wines are unfairly neglected by the national wine press. Although Osberger was in no way implicated by the scandal, the events of 1985 hit him hard: before that time he was exporting as much as 65 percent of his production; now the figure is nearer five percent. He is justifiably bitter; as his son says, "the scandal was caused by 20 people and ruined 35,000 people who earned their livelihoods from Austrian wine!"

The Osbergers have been winemakers in Strass since 1785 and every generation they seem to take over a bit more of the swollen village. As Helmut Osberger junior says, "It is a principal of the family that an Osberger should leave behind him good equipment, good vineyards and progeny to ensure the continued prosperity of the dynasty." Osberger provides some interesting services for wine lovers: he sells wine going back to 1956 which he can ship anywhere in the world inside ten days (Helmut senior walled up the old cellar as the Russians approached and saved stocks going back to 1923); he will also guarantee the wines from his vineyards for 15 years. Osberger challenges Lenz Moser's dictum: "the best wine is that which is sold", with his own: "the best advice is good provision".

Old wine is, indeed, the house speciality: Osberger does not approve of the post-1985 trend to drink ever-younger wines, "it's like sending your children down the pit", he says. Osberger produces anything between 200 and 300 wines each vintage, ranging from his reliable gastronomic range of *Fischwein* and *Wildwein* (wines for fish and game) to his top wines from the Heiligenstein and other *crus*. The Rhine Riesling is certainly one of his best; tightly made to age as demonstrated by the 1989 and 1986. Only the 1977 showed the real potential, with its rose-petal aromas. Osberger makes some good *Prädikat* wines such as his 1975 Malvasier Auslese or an exquisite 1979 Muskat Ottonel Trockenbeerenauslese. From the Osberger orchards come some fine schnapps, the best being a Nussbrand (nut schnapps) for which the walnuts are macerated in blackcurrant schnapps. Osberger recommends its digestive qualities.

Vineyards on the valley floor of the Kamptal.

Johann Topf is Osberger's son-in-law, but one does not get the impression that they often see eye to eye. Topf's best wines are his Weissburgunders but with time his Chardonnays could become equally good. The former are splendidly nutty and older vintages going back to 1970 attest to their staying power. Topf has had some teething problems in getting the oak right in his Chardonnays; the 1990s are certainly the best to date, now that he has toned down the Manhartsberg oak a little and used more subtle Allier barrels.

Peter Dolle is another Strasser winemaker with a collection of old wines in his beautifully designed modern cellar. Dolle's family came from eastern Germany after the war and only gradually moved from agriculture to viticulture. They now cultivate some 20 hectares (quite large by Austrian standards). Part of the wine is sold in the very *gemütlichen* (cosy) *Buschenschank* done up with chintzy decorations including lacy slogans of the "*Mein Heim mein Alles*" (home sweet home) ilk.

Dolle occasionally goes overboard on the acidity; his 1987 Sauvignon Blanc being a case in point: alcohol 11.2 percent, acidity 11.8 g/l. Wines of this sort probably bring on stomach ulcers. Fortunately they are not all so extreme: Grüner Veltliners are best from the Ried Strasser Gaisberg with their tinned pea-soup character; while Rhine Rieslings from the Brunngasse can be very classy. The Weissburgunders are better than the Chardonnays here, and there are even some lovely 1976s still to be had.

The last of our Strasser quartet is the **Metternich'sche Weingüter**; a cousin of Schloss Johannisberg in the Rheingau, owned by another Metternich. Sadly old wine stocks here at Schloss Grafenegg could not be defended as easily as they were *chez* Osberger: the Russians chose the *Schloss* as their command HQ and made a point of wrecking the cellar as soon as they had drunk it dry. The *Schloss* is essentially a late mediaeval building, much altered in the last century. The old wine cellar is under the chapel, with the best wines occupying the spaces designed for Metternich coffins.

The Metternich'sche Weingüter is now run as a sort of nobleman's cooperative along with the Esterhazy estate in Eisenstadt, the Starhemberg estate in the Kremstal, the Abensperg-Traun estate in Maissau (Weinviertel) and the Khevenhüller-Metsch estate in Pulkau. There are 65 hectares in all. At Metternich everything is aged in steel, and some wines are kept in steel for a number of years before release. I must say that I am a little baffled by this policy, as it seems to prove only that wines are perfectly inert in these conditions and neither age nor develop. All it means is that you have to age what are already quite old wines yourself before they are ready to drink!

Grüner Veltliner leads the field: the young wines are fresh, clean and lentilly, while a 1981 Auslese came as a surprise with its honey-and-apples fruit. Müller-Thurgau is a good bet here: I recall a

Left: The volcanic soils of Zöbing with the Manhartsberg behind. The oak from Manhartsberg is highly praised.
Above: Picking grapes in the Kamptal.

Riesling-like 1979 which was excellent. Of the Rieslings themselves, the best are from the Ried Kreuzberg in Krems.

The Mantlerhof is in Brunn im Felde in the Kaiserstiege sub-region of Kamptal-Donauland. It is here that **Sepp Mantler** makes a speciality of the rare Roter Veltliner. The Roter Veltliner, or Roter Muskateller as it used to be known, was formerly a dominant variety in these parts. Like all 'red' varieties in Austria, it makes white wine. Red wine in Austria comes from 'blue' grapes; the Roter Veltliner is 'red' because the grapes turn skin-pink when they are ripe.

The Roter Veltliner can make delicious wines in the hands of an expert such as Sepp Mantler. It has more extract than its green cousin and is more susceptible to *Botrytis* (both the noble and ignoble sorts). With age it tends to earthiness, like Mantler's 1989s and 1988s from the Ried Reisenthal. The latter was an excellent year for the Roter Veltliner and the grapes were picked at *Auslese* levels. Mantler also made big, spicy Roter Veltliners in 1987 and 1986, of which the latter is a triumph with its spicy, peachy fruit. In 1983 he made an *Ausbruch* tasting of cooked plums and peaches.

Sepp Mantler is known as Austria's only Roter Veltliner specialist. However, he does also make excellent Grüner Veltliners which are perhaps overlooked. Some of these also come from the Ried Reisenthal.

The town of Langenlois in the Kamptal once disputed with Gols in Burgenland the title of Austria's largest wine commune. After many years the argument was patched up to everyone's satisfaction when it was decided that Langenlois would be 'Austria's greatest wine town' while Gols should be 'Austria's greatest wine village'. There are now fewer stormy scenes in the Loch Ness pub (Langenlois' most racy night-spot) on a Saturday night, and the town has lapsed into its more fitting and habitual torpor.

The key to Langenlois' quality as a wine-producing area is the south-facing amphitheatre of hills which surround the town. **Ludwig Hiedler** has now taken over the winemaking from his father, Dr Bruno Hiedler, on the family's 21-hectare estate (seven hectares are made up of contract growers)

based in a charming old house in the centre of town (opposite the Loch Ness) where his Spanish-born wife Maria looks after the office work. Ludwig Hiedler is a very careful winemaker and his dedication at all levels of the process is apparent in his wines. The only wine I would fault in the whole collection would be the Zweigelt that he makes to accomodate Austrian demand for red wines. His loess- and loam-grown Grüner Veltliners are quite superb, as are the Rhine Rieslings which he grows on a particularly steep slope to give them a wonderful acidity and length. The family *Liebkind* is the Weissburgunder which, when late-picked, produces wines of great nutty intensity. There is also a promising Chardonnay. Hiedler has not yet jumped on the new-oak band-wagon and ferments his wine in big tuns of Acacia wood.

The Sonnhof estate is another domaine housed in an old cloistral building with fine, ancient cellars. The **Jurtschitsch** family acquired the property and its 23 hectares of vines during the war and it is now run by three brothers: Edwin, Paul and Karl.

The Jurtschitsch cellars are filled with mod cons and this helps to make zingy-fresh Grüner Veltliners, especially those from the Ried Steinhaus, which in this case seem to age with dignity. In 1986, the brothers picked a Grüner Veltliner on 5 December and fermented it in new oak! The results were strangely delicious. My favourite Jurtschitsch wines are the primary rock Rieslings, of which I tasted a brilliant series going back to 1979. Their latest passion is a red wine called Rotspon, which is now made from 80 percent Blauburgunder and 20 percent Zweigelt, the Zweigelt having taken the place of Blaufränkisch. The wine is really a Pinot Noir with a little extra colour and aroma provided by the secondary variety. The wine goes into (a little too much) new oak. The best vintages are 1985, 1986 and 1988.

If one had to choose one producer who exemplified the 'new wave' in Austrian wine it would be the younger **Willi Bründlmayer**. Bründlmayer is an internationalist by training: he studied economics in Austria, and winemaking in Geisenheim, West Germany, before going on to gain practical experience in Burgundy and Switzerland. His wines bear the hallmark of one who has seen things at first hand and who knows precisely how they are achieved.

The Jurtschitsch cellars in Langenlois. New oak barrels lie alongside a collection of the estate's best wines.

The Jurtschitschs produce fresh, steely Rieslings and Grüner Veltliners using their expensive high-tech equipment.

Paradoxically, however, the Bründlmayers remain firmly rooted in Langenlois where the family has made wine since the seventeenth century. There are now about 45 hectares planted, making it one of Austria's largest private domaines. It is typically Austrian in its refusal to specialise in any particular grape and in young Willi's insistence on using the local Manhartsberg oak to age his highly successful wines.

Again it would be hard to select only a few of Bründlmayer's excellent wines: the Grüner Veltliner from Loiser Berg Vogelsang is grown on granite. Bründlmayer calls it "a perfect vineyard with excellent ageing potential". This he proceeded to prove with a 1985 with a rich, nutty character followed by a 1983 Spätlese with delicious, peachy fruit. From the Zöbinger Heiligenstein comes his best Rhine Riesling; this is slightly broader than the Wachau style with a richer fruitiness. In 1979 he made an exciting Beerenauslese from this wine.

Neither Grüner Veltliner nor Riesling sees oak, but this is not the case for the Burgunders. Bründlmayer makes one *cuvée* in which he mixes Ruländer and Weissburgunder. In another he ferments the Ruländer in new Manhartsberg oak which gives it a rich acacia-honey and butter taste. Bründlmayer's Chardonnay is possibly the best Austrian attempt at the international Chardonnay style. In hot years such as 1990 the wine does not undergo malolactic fermentation. It is, however, always fermented in 100 percent new Manhartsberg oak, giving it that intense, butter-and-bananas character in its youth. The 1985 shows the wine in maturity: it has shed some of its new oak flavours and evolved more orange, peach and aniseed; a lovely wine.

Bründlmayer makes two red-wine *cuvées*: Cecile and Vincent (named after his children). Cecile is Blauburgunder with a little Merlot to give colour and extra aromas: in years such as 1983 this can be a really superb wine, full of chunky red fruits with a slight hint of dill. The Vincent is a blend of Cabernet Sauvignon, Cabernet Franc and Merlot; there is a slight grassiness about this wine, which must result from the rather cool climate in Langenlois for Bordeaux-style wines. Bründlmayer, however, is optimistic; he says that the climate is going to get hotter over the next 50 years. Once again it was the Blauburgunder which impressed me most; this comes from the Ried Dechant. The 1989 is full of chocolate and raisins, while a mature 1979 exuded rose petals and violets with that slight earthiness associated with Pinot Noir. I also remember with great pleasure a 1975 from an ill-starred vintage, with that same cocoa character which made an astonishing comeback during a meal at the Altwienerhof restaurant in Vienna.

DONAULAND-CARNUNTUM

Donauland-Carnuntum is a large, amorphous region which stretches all the way from St Pòlten in the west to the frontier by Bratislava (Pressburg). One would be hard pressed to find any general characteristics for the area except to say that it falls either side of Vienna and either side of the River Danube. The Carnuntum of the name refers to the old Roman city which lies to the far east, not so distant from the border, and which is known for its surviving Roman triumphal arch. The inclusion of Carnuntum in the title of the region is yet another bone of contention: "we're about as near Carnuntum as we are to Linz!" says an exasperated Ludwig Neumayer in Inzersdorf. Recently there have been a few rumours that the government is planning to split the area in two.

If Donauland-Carnuntum had such a thing as a focal point it would be the old city of Klosterneuburg to the west of Vienna. The city grew up in the shadow of the ancient monastery of Klosterneuburg mentioned in Chapter One (*see p* 12). The **monks of Klosterneuburg** are still in residence (at least a few of them are) and they constitute the largest vineyard owner in Austria with their 103 hectares (compare Château Margaux: 85 hectares; Château Lafite: 90 hectares!).

The monastic vines fall into three packets in three different regions: some are, strictly speaking, in Vienna; others are in Donauland-Carnuntum proper; while the third, partly red-wine producing section, is in Gumpoldskirchen and Tattendorf in the Thermenregion. The Viennese vines are all planted on the steep slopes of the Kahlenberg, the last of the city's western hills. The best wines from the Viennese vineyards are the Weissburgunders from the Ried Kuchelviertel, with their aromas of honey and peaches. A rare 1981 Auslese proves that these wines develop even greater intensity at *Prädikat* level. Some heady Gewürztraminer is produced from vineyards on the Ried Gebhardin.

In Klosterneuburg, the Grüner Veltliner from the Ried Wiegen put me in mind of a pea-soup with bacon! Here the Rieslings from Ried Steinriegel and Franzhauser seem to produce the classiest wines with their intense limes and petrol fruit. A

The restored romanesque abbey-church in Klosterneuburg.

Neuburger Trockenbeerenauslese 1967 from the Ried Franzhauser was a real discovery with its intense nutty character. One of the joys of Klosterneuburg is that a good many of these old wines are still on sale from the monastery shop.

From Tattendorf in the Thermenregion come good St-Laurents, the best of which are graced with the title *Ausstich* (literally sampled out). The 1988s were successful here, with good depth of raspberry-scented fruit coming from the Ried Stiftsbreite. A small amount is now aged in small oak to give it the oaky aromas so much in demand from Austrian customers.

Near to Carnuntum itself, the village of Göttlesbrunn benefits from a hot, dry climate not dissimilar to that of Burgenland to the south. Göttlesbrunn is currently being shaken up by a couple of wine-mad local vets who have made huge strides to get local growers to be aware of quality wine. Wine evenings in the village are organised and played out with all the solemnity of a prayer meeting, while the growers en masse dissect the imponderables of quality. That these sessions have an effect is obvious from the wines themselves: the overall quality is very high indeed.

Walter Glatzer is the son of the mayor of Göttlesbrunn, an ardent young man, in many ways typical of the village winemakers. Glatzer came to the fore with his 1990s when he made a fine Dornenvogel Grüner Veltliner and some lovely Weissburgunders, notably the dry Spätlese and the Kabinett. His Zweigelt Dornenvogel is another wine to look out for.

Göttlesbrunn's most eccentric winemaker is **Johann Messermayer**. Messermayer possesses a cellar full of ancient goodies all piled up willy-nilly with no apparent attempt at order. He is a considerable devotee of his own wine and enjoys the odd tipple. There are indeed some fine things here, such as his 1990 Grüner Veltliners and Rhine Rieslings (I should add that Göttlesbrunn is not particularly famous for either variety). Messermayer also has stocks of old Weissburgunders and Traminers, among which one can find the occasional treasure.

Hans Pitnauer is the best winemaker in Göttlesbrunn. He seems to be constantly experimenting with something, and in general the results are exciting. Take, for example, his Weiss aus Rot, a white wine made from black grapes quickly removed from their skins; or his Franz Josef Zweigelt/St-Laurent blend; his Bienenfresser (Bee-eater) grappa and six-year-old brandy; or indeed his remarkably convincing (and extremely good value) vermouth made from Grüner Veltliner! In a more serious vein, Pitnauer's best whites are his Weissburgunders, such as the 1986 which came top in the regional show and the 1989, which in my opinion is even better with its slightly *botrytised* creaminess. Pitnauer's secret is late picking; the aridity of the climate here allows him to wait until November to get the full goodness from his grapes. His reds are full and dense, especially his St-Laurents and Zweigelts. The latter are bottled under the Bienenfresser label.

Not far from Göttlesbrunn, in the commune of Höflein, is the estate of the **Artner** family. The Artners have been clever at selling their wines into fashionable Viennese restaurants and clubs so that their name commands a certain reputation in the capital. Wine is only part of their interests as they also own a certain amount of farmland. Artner's best wines are the unoaked whites: Grüner Veltliner (including a well-preserved 1986) and Welschriesling. They also make an impressive unoaked Blauer Portugieser.

Wagram is an area which lies to the north of the Danube and some kilometres to the west of Vienna. At the centre lies Kirchberg am Wagram and from there it is only a short distance to Oberstockstall with its marvellous Renaissance *Schloss*. Wagram is

Vines in the Wagram area of Donauland-Carnuntum. In the distance is the Renaissance Schloss *of Oberstockstall, housing a restaurant.*

Inzersdorf in the region of Donauland-Carnuntum; this is the home of Ludwig Neumayer; one of the rising stars of Austrian winemaking.

much more a Grüner Veltliner region than Göttlesbrunn and the best wines of **Karl Fritsch** are his Veltliners. Some of the wine is vinified in a light style and given the name of *Windspiel*, in imitation of the *Federspiel* of the Wachau (*see p* 46). Personally, I prefer the more conventionally vinified and less acidic Veltliners. Fritsch also makes some good Zweigelt.

Franz Leth has a comparatively large estate in Fels am Wagram. He admits to growing "virtually every variety of grape" and buys in grapes and wine as well. With such a large business quality is occasionally dodgy, but there are some good things for all that: a Wagram Selection Grüner Veltliner with an authentic lentil character; a Frühroter Veltliner with a luscious, peachy/apricoty fruitiness; and a surprisingly authentic-tasting Rhine Riesling grown on sandy loam. Leth's Gelber Muskateller is also good with a powerful scent of roses in the 1989 vintage; while a 1986 Traminer had big, lemon-curd character. In 1989 Leth made a decent, if one-dimensional Blauburgunder.

The current star of the whole Donauland-Carnuntum region is **Ludwig Neumayer**, who runs a 5.5-hectare family estate in the far west of the region in Inzersdorf. Ludwig Neumayer started making wine seriously only in 1985, realising both

his own dream and that of his banker brother. His ascent has been meteoric: now many of Austria's best restaurants stock Neumayer wines and consequently there is little left to supply private customers.

It comes as a bit of a surprise to find good wine in a place like Inzersdorf. For miles around the villages are distinguished only by the strong smell of pigs which emanates from the farm courtyards. Yet, as the Neumayers point out so eloquently, the soil here is good primary rock. This shows in the wines, for example the Grüner Veltliner from Ried Zwirch, which in the 1990 vintage had wonderfully ripe, lentilly fruit. The Rhine Riesling vom Stein is another highly refined wine which could be safely put away for many years and continue to improve. From the same *Ried* Neumayer makes a fine Weissburgunder and a very good Chardonnay which was very fat and peachy in the 1990 vintage. The brothers are not tempted by *barriques* for the present, revealing fully their cautious policy – not that the wine needed the wood, it was perfectly rounded and full of fruit flavour. Neumayer does not make sweet wines, but in the best years he makes a dry *Auslese* from his grapes. His 1986 Grüner Veltliner and Weissburgunder are highly successful wines of this genre.

WEINVIERTEL

Much like the region of Donauland-Carnuntum, the Weinviertel is an uneasy gathering of regions, each of which formerly possessed an established identity. To the extreme west is Retz, the driest corner of Austria's wine country with an average annual rainfall of under 350mm and a permanent wind which ensures that the area around the pretty old town is never visited by the likes of *Botrytis cinerea*. Retz is a red wine region, as to some extent are the Pulkau Valley and the Mailberg area to the east. Around Röschitz and Hollabrunn the Grüner Veltliner is typical, often showing a smoky character from the primary rock soils; Grüner Veltliner also predominates in the areas of Poysdorf and Falkenstein in the east of the region, where a comparatively damp climate creates wines of better aromatic character. Finally in the far southeast of the Weinviertel the aridity returns as the land touches the Pannonian regions of eastern Donauland-Carnuntum.

Mannersdorf an der March is on Austria's eastern border with Czecho-Slovakia. On the top of the Kellerberg hill is the Rochus-Kapelle, a pretty seventeenth-century imitation of the Bramante Tempietto in Rome built to commemorate the end of the Thirty Years War. Only a few metres from this is the cellar of **Roland Minkowitsch**, the best-known grower in the village.

Minkowitsch is the son of a former president of the Austrian Federal Parliament who learned his winemaking in South Africa. More than a third of his vines are Rhine Riesling, which he bottles under the De Vite label. Older vintages of De Vite used to contain Neuburger, but now they are pure Riesling. These Rieslings are surprisingly angular in this Pannonian corner of the Weinviertel, with authentic lime and honey aromas occasionally enhanced by a whiff of lavender. Minkowitsch is also a capable craftsman with his Welschriesling grapes and makes wines with good, fruity character for a change. In 1988 he made a rare *Ausbruch* from *Botrytis*-affected grapes. Look out also for his Gewürztraminers.

The village of Stetten is not so far from Vienna, on the far side of the same Bisamberg on which some of the city's best wines are grown. The top

grower in Stetten is undoubtedly **Roman Pfaffl**. Pfaffl seems to live in olfactory cohabitation with his neighbour's horse, but the smell of this animal is kept out of his smart new tasting room. Pfaffl subscribes to the current fashionable ideas about acidity, which means that his wines can be a little searing for the uninitiated. Pfaffl's Grüner Veltliners from the Ried Haidviertel, Hundsleiten and Zieseneck are all rather austere and angular but extremely well made. A small amount of Grüner Veltliner is put into new oak, which I find unconvincing; oak and Veltliner do not mix. Pfaffl made some pleasant Zweigelt reds in 1988 and 1989.

The old road to the Bohemian city of Brünn (Brno in Czech) bisects the eastern half of the Weinviertel. The road gave its name to a style of wine in the old days, when *Brünnerstrassler* was synonymous with sharp, acidic white wines. Better winemaking techniques in our own century have tamed the ferocious acidity of the *Brünnerstrassler*, but it is still in demand for the big Sekt producers who value the clean, neutral fruit they can get from this area. **Josef Pleil's** small estate is in Wolkersdorf at the beginning of the Brünnerstrasse, so close to Vienna that on a clear day you can see Saint Stephan's Cathedral. In Wolkersdorf there are as many as 1,000 hectares of vines, the produce of which chiefly goes to the cooperative cellar.

The best wines of Wolkersdorf have the right to a specific Grüner Hahn label which is permitted only for the top varietal wines. Pleil leads on his Grüner Veltliners; nice sappy wines which show an occasional fresh-pea aroma which turns to sorrel in the older vintages. Also good are Pleil's Welschrieslings, in which he tries to get as much fruit as possible out of the grape – the 1986 in particular was showered with medals at Austrian shows. He makes a small amount of Blaufränkisch, of which the 1988 was the most successful recent vintage.

The Brünnerstrasse proceeds from Wolkersdorf to Höbersbrunn, where the curiously named **Josef Leberwurst** makes his award-winning wines, and then on to Poysdorf before coming up against the Czech frontier. As you enter Poysdorf you pass a sign which reads *"Schlumberger Sekt: aus Poysdorfer Wein hergestellt"* (Schlumberger Sekt: produced from Poysdorf wine). This region provides the base wines for the big Sekt cellars.

Right: The Biedermayer offices of Kattus in Vienna.
Below: Many Sekt base wines come from the Poysdorf region.

The main offices of the Sekt companies are in the western suburbs of Vienna where they were established in the first half of the last century (*see p 26*). **Schlumberger** occupies an enormous warren of cellars in Döbling. The wines made by the *méthode champenoise* are produced from the grapes of 250 farmers in the Poysdorf area. All the export quality wines are hand riddled. The dominant grape variety in Austrian sparkling-wine production is the Welschriesling. This grape makes rather neutral, highly acidic wines, their chief virtue being cleanliness. However, Schlumberger makes one Sekt from Weissburgunder: Cuvée Victoria; for me this is their most characterful wine with plenty of fruit. Schlumberger also owns the old house of Mounier which produces some interesting Sekt made from the Rhine Riesling grape.

Not far from Schlumberger are the Biedermeyer offices of **Johann Kattus**, where the sparkling wines are made by the transfer method rather than the bottle-fermented *méthode champenoise* practised by Schlumberger. Kattus Sekts contain a higher proportion of Grüner Veltliner than their rivals and, apart from the Grosser Jahrgang Brut, they all have higher levels of residual sugar, making them a better partner for the sort of sticky cakes you find in the average Viennese *Konditorei*. One of the chief virtues of Kattus is the lovely Jugendstil labels mentioned in Chapter I (*see p 26*) which still proclaim the firm as the official supplier to the Habsburg court (which disappeared more than 70 years ago).

One grower in Poysdorf who has nothing to do with Sekt production is **Helmut Taubenschuss**. Behind the rather bland exterior of his house in the town, Taubenschuss inhabits a ravishing 'Frankish' collonaded courtyard where he matures the wines from his ten hectares of vines. Taubenschuss gets superb concentration from his vines by performing a rigourous *vendange verte*: he discards whole bunches of grapes in the summer to feed all the goodness of the vines into a few selected clusters. This also means that the alcohol levels here are higher than is usually the case in Poysdorf, and the acidity correspondingly more tolerable.

Helmut Taubenschuss' Frankish courtyard in Poysdorf.
Taubenschuss makes some of the region's most exciting wines.

Taubenschuss's best wines are his Weissbur-gunders; far more interesting in my opinion than his Chardonnay, but time may reverse this judgement. He made great wines from this grape in 1983, 1986, 1988, 1989 and 1990. In that last vintage he also produced a series of big, sappy Grüner Veltliners.

On the other side of Poysdorf are the cellars of **Emmerich Haimer**. Haimer makes rather smoky-flavoured Grüner Veltliners in a style more reminiscent of Retz than Poysdorf; both the 1990s and the 1989s were particularly good. Also good are Haimer's Roter Traminer (ie Gewürztraminer – some Austrian Gewürztraminer is yellow when ripe, hence the quibble) with their honey, rose-petal and lavender aromas. As elsewhere, Haimer benefited from the very long growing season in 1990 to make a sweet wine, in this case a splendid *Eiswein* with 104 grams of residual sugar, picked on 4 December.

The Weinviertel has its *Eiswein* specialist in **Fritz Rieder** of Kleinhadersdorf, or Weinrieder as he likes to be known. Except in the southeast, the Weinviertel is too dry to allow for *Botrytis cinerea* to develop on the vines and the only solution, if growers want a high *Prädikat* wine, is to take a chance on the frosts and hope that the starlings have left you enough grapes to make some *Eiswein*. Rieder is possibly the only man in Austria who tries to make *Eiswein* year in year out in commercial quantities. It is a process which must require remarkable patience: in the 1990 vintage he actually harvested his last grapes on the first day of the Gulf War (16 January).

Rieder makes his *Eiswein* from any healthy grapes which remain on the vines at the end of the growing season. Unlike a *Beerenauslese* or *Trocken-beerenauslese*, *Eiswein* retains a strong imprint of the grape variety, so that the vulgarity of certain cultivars (Bouvier and Scheurebe spring instantly to mind) is immediately apparent. Rieder's best come from the Welschriesling and Neuburger grapes. In 1988 he made one *Eiswein* from some Welschriesling grapes which had actually died on the vine; producing some really strange aromas in the finished wine. Rieder is passionate about this brew.

Not far from Poysdorf is the picturesque village of Falkenstein dominated by its church and ruined *Schloss*. Falkenstein has one of the best *Kellergassen* in Lower Austria, from which there is a superb view of the castle. It is here that the cellars of **Heinrich Salomon** are to be found. Salomon made some very fine Grüner Veltliners and Rhine Rieslings in the 1990 vintage. Anyone interested in this wine should know that the best of the Grüner Veltliners were released under the Falkensteiner Berggericht label.

In the less romantic *Kellergasse* on the other side of the village, **Reinhard Neustifter** has his cluttered little cellar. Besides some very good, concentrated Grüner Veltliners, Neustifter is to be remembered for some remarkably intense Weissburgunders which he seems able to succeed with,

Church, vines and ruined castle at Falkenstein.

even in generally poor years like 1987. The 1990 dry Spätlese is particularly promising.

Josef Strell is in the western half of the Weinviertel, in Radlbrunn, to the north of Wagram. His is a 'green' vineyard, which may account for the truly remarkable number of insects which take refuge in his cellar. Of course, the insects might be wine lovers, for Strell has some remarkably good things down there: some intense Grüner Veltliners from the Ried Lehen; greengage-scented Weissburgunders from the Ried Karln (the 1969 is a real treasure); and some superb unoaked Chardonnays. Strell put some of his 1990 Chardonnay into new Allier barrels for far too long, making a wine which tasted of nothing more than oak; his 1989 Chardonnay demonstrates a more reasoned policy: a little oak-aged wine is added to that aged in large tuns. Strell also makes some chunky Zweigelts with surprisingly good ageing potential.

Near the lovely old walled town of Eggenburg, with its baroque gables, is the village of Röschitz.

Here on the primary rock soils are grown some of Austria's most typical Grüner Veltliners – so typical, in fact, that the locals refer to the grape as the "*Urveltliner*" (original Veltliner). A good producer of classic, lentils-and-white-pepper Veltliners is **Ernst Kölbl**. Many of the local growers bind themselves to local quality organisations which are grouped under a plethora of bewildering names: **Matthias Corvinus** (young winemakers); **Vinumvirat** (three growers including the younger Kölbl, Franz Prechtl and Norbert Bauer) and **Collegium Vini Cultorum**, growers from the Röschitz region whose white wines grow on the primary rocks of the Bohemian hills and who use the distinctive Feenhaube label.

Werner Zull in Schrattenthal is another member of the Collegium Vini Cultorum. Schrattenthal is a rather unprepossessing sort of place, in many ways typical of the gloomier villages of Lower Austria and relieved only by the fact that it possesses a grower by the name of **Leopold Wurst** and the excellent Grüner Veltliners and Rhine Rieslings of Werner Zull. In Schrattenthal, growers experiment with red wines as well as white. The neighbouring village of Zellerndorf is actually situated in the Pulkau valley, which has long been famed as a centre of red wine production. In Zellerndorf the **Prechtl** family make some fine wines from the generally dull Blauer Portugieser.

In nearby Haugsdorf is a superlative red winemaker in the person of **Josef Lust**. Lust has two large cellars in Haugsdorf's magnificent *Kellergasse*, where the buildings, each emblazoned with a winemaker's family name, resemble the bourgeois tombs of a smart French cemetery. Lust's best Blauer Portugiesers from the Ried Aussatzen, as well as his Exklusive label, have lovely, dense raspberry fruit and a concentrated, chocolaty finish. His best Blauburgers come from the Ried Sonnen and these have a strong blackcurrant aroma. They last too: a 1983 Portugieser was violet-scented and charming; a 1979 Blauburger full of toasty, buttery, strawberry fruit. Lust also makes a Portugieser/Blauburger blend which he puts into new oak from the appropriately named Glaswein forest.

Lenz Moser is possibly the only Austrian wine name to be known throughout the world. I am old

Old vintages in the Lenz Moser cellars at Rohrendorf.

enough to remember the baroque labels of Schluck, Lenz Moser IV's immensely popular white wine which used to grace the shelves of every British supermarket. Schluck fell victim to the witchhunt which followed the wine scandal, and the present Lenz Moser administration, headed by Lenz Moser V, fights shy of the branded market, preferring to bottle its 'Selection' of wines bought from small growers, chiefly in Burgenland. Lenz Moser Weinkellerei also rents the Klosterkeller Siegendorf in Burgenland.

Rohrendorf, where the Mosers have their fief, is actually in Kamptal-Donauland. The main offices sit on top of one thousand-year-old cellars which contain the largest tun in Austria, specially commissioned by Hermann Göring because he was jealous of the canons of Klosterneuburg. The first Moser arrived in the area not long after the construction of the cellars and the firm was established in 1849. The first Lenz (short for Laurenz) joined the company in 1880.

Lenz Moser V sees the firm as "a red wine house", at least as far as their vines in the Weinviertel are concerned. These are rented from the Knights of Malta, hence the name: Malteser Ritterorden. The Malteser Ritterorden reds are generally very classy wines. The Zweigelt starts the range; in a good year such as 1990 it is a big mouthful of red fruits. The Blauburgunders have good, authentic burgundian aromas (I have noted "violets grown on a compost heap" beside the 1988) but less of the Pinot Noir texture than, say, Bründlmayer. Lenz Moser V's pride and joy is his Cabernet/Merlot blend; one of the first wines of its sort in Austria and one which is eagerly grubbed up by wine lovers as soon as it is released onto the market.

Red wine also accounts for the fame of the **Landwirtschaftliche Fachschule Retz** (generally just called the Weinbauschule, or WBS for short). The reputation of the Retz wine school is to a very great degree the work of Gerhard Redl, who is responsible for teaching vinification techniques. Redl has influenced a whole generation of winemakers in Austria; not just locals like the younger Gruber or fellow teacher Walter Pollak in nearby Unterretzbach, but men and women as far away as Burgenland. Redl is really Austria's greatest redwine pundit, and he uses the school's 12-hectare vineyard on the granite hills outside Retz to demonstrate just how good red wines can be from this arid corner of Austria.

The Altenberg is a winemaker's playground. Redl plants something different all the time. Recently he latched onto *macération carbonique* and is anxious to try it out on some Gamay that he has put down. In 1992 he is planting Syrah, as he feels that the granite soils of the Altenberg could produce some interesting results with the Rhône variety.

The most famous red wine from the school is Granat, a blend of 90 percent Blauer Portugieser with some ten percent Merlot. The popularity of this wine gives Redl the chance to concentrate on his experiments, chiefly his Cabernet Sauvignon/ Cabernet Franc blend. Redl took some trouble to get expensive French clones for this wine, which excites a good deal of curiosity from Austrian wine drinkers for whom Cabernet is some sort of Nirvana. Yet again, I prefer other wines, such as Ergo, a Blauburger housed in buttery Glaswein oak and, most of all, his Blauburgunder. I have tasted only two vintages of this wine: a smoky, raspberry-scented 1983, which lacked classic Pinot Noir texture, and an excellent 1989 which was as authentic a Blauburgunder as I have found in Austria. Once again it seems to point Austria towards this tricky but rewarding grape variety.

*Above: A Renaissance house in the
square of Retz with sgraffito decoration.
Top: The church tower above the market
square in Retz. The town is notable for
its network of underground wine cellars.
Left: The Altenberg vineyard, owned by
the Retz wine school. The town is in the
background.*

THERMENREGION

Thermenregion was one of the very last regions of Austria to recover from the fall-out of the wine scandal. The principal reason for this is linked to the village of Gumpoldskirchen in the north of the Südbahn, as the area used to be called (the decision to change the name was doubtless based on the need to rethink the reputation of the villages around the spa towns of Baden and Bad Vöslau). Gumpolds-kirchen had long thrived on its semi-sweet white wines made from two local grapes: the Zierfandler and the Rotgipfler. In an average year these two produced wines with decent *Prädikat* levels but no noble rot; the sort of wine which was being aped by the 1985 fraudsters. Naturally these were the wines which went out of fashion first after 1985. For a while the picturesque streets of Gumpoldskirchen were robbed of their usual bus-loads of German and Japanese tourists. The big men in the local trade were ruined and those growers who were not prepared to diversify or fight for their wines took early retirement and sold off their vines.

Two of the men who decided that the time had come to change the style of wines associated with the region are **Gottfried Schellmann** and **Manfred Biegler**. Schellmann's response to the problem was to replant his seven hectares of vines and concentrate increasingly on dry white wines.

Baden is renowned for its ornate 19th-century villas; these were constructed after the town achieved popularity as a spa.

Chardonnay is Schellmann's *Liebkind* and he has managed to achieve a reputation in a very short time for these wines. Schellmann has also planted some Rhine Riesling which produces rather fat, apricot-scented wines in the rolling hills of Gum-poldskirchen. I still feel that his best wines come from the core of old Zierfandler and Rotgipfler vines he has preserved; here the 1990 was the best vintage since 1986. Schellmann vinifies some of the Rotgipfler as a dry wine, but with time these put on weight and develop exciting brown-bread tastes, combined with aromas of stewed rhubarb.

On the other side of Gumpoldskirchen's main street is Manfred Biegler. Biegler is currently rep-lanting Zierfandler vines as the climate of opinion is now beginning to change in favour of the authentic style of the region. He has some Weissburgunder and Rhine Riesling, but his best wines are almost all made from the traditional Gumpoldskirchner grapes or from the Neuburger, which is the most widely planted variety taking the region as a whole. His most recent Zierfandlers and Rotgipflers have been vinified dry or half dry and some of his wines are now put into small oak barrels for a few months.

There are still a few men about in Gumpoldskir-chen who were never tempted to change their style of winemaking. One of these is **Josef Weiss**, whose small estate contained, until recently, only Zier-fandler, Rotgipfler and a small amount of Neu-burger. Now he has added a little Welschriesling and Rhine Riesling, but one does not get the impression that he is particularly convinced by these varieties. Weiss's Rotgipfler and Zierfandler *Spätlese* wines from the 1990 vintage should evolve into something every bit as good as some of his earlier successes; notably in the 1982, 1979 and 1976 vintages.

Friedrich Hofer cuts a curious figure in his kaleidoscopic, fluorescent tracksuit. This startling outfit might lead one to believe that Hofer was a modernist, but the truth is quite the reverse: Hofer actually specialises in sweet wines which he still presses on an old-fashioned horizontal press. The advantage of this, he says, is that the press does not extract so much, leaving all the goodness in the juice rather than pulp. Hofer led us out into the vineyard behind his house to show us some ripen-ing grapes; the Zierfandler was demonstrating why

it is also sometimes called Spätrot: the berries
having turned quite pink at the beginning of
October. The Rotgipfler, by the way, gets its name
from the red stems which appear in the spring.

Hofer also has some Neuburger which makes
typically nutty, fat wines on his soils; but it is with
the Rotgipfler and Zierfandler that he excels. His
1989 Rotgipfler Auslese is one of the best post-1985
Gumpoldskirchners I have tasted and the 1990
Zierfandler Auslese is not far behind. A 1986
Rotgipfler Beerenauslese 1986, with its intense
brown-bread and spiced-apricot character, was
enough to show just what these wines can do with a
little bottle-age.

Another man who is voluble on the subject of the
real nature of Gumpoldskirchen is **Franz Kurz**.
Kurz is convinced that the time has come to lead the
wine-loving public back to Zierfandler and Rotgipfler. Kurz also sets himself high targets for his
Prädikat wines, saying that a *Spätlese* must have
21° KMW and an *Auslese* 23° (as opposed to 19° and
21°). It is in these categories that he excels, with
wines like his Zierfandler Auslese 1990 and 1986.
His most highly acclaimed wine to date is the
superb Trockenbeerenauslese he made from Spä-
trot/Rotgipfler in 1989. Just 650 small bottles of
this elixir were filled.

The wines of Traiskirchen have never been pris-
oners of their own image in the way that Gumpoldskirchen's have. The village (more of a town
really) is rather ugly and few tourists come here.
This possibly encourages winemakers to spend
more time in their vineyards and press-houses and
less with their customers. Which is not to say that
they do not possess *Buschenschenken*; they all do,
but they are rather more serious affairs.

When I met **Karl Alphart** he was somewhat
preoccupied with his vintage. His vines lie partly
on the steeper hillsides towards Gumpoldskirchen
and partly on the plain. This allows him to make a
stylish Riesling on a chalky slope which was pre-
viously reserved for Zierfandler. About a third of
Alphart's wines are Neuburger, which he uses to
make anything from a dry wine to an *Auslese*. From
his best sites, such as the Ried Steinfeld and Haus-
berg, the Neuburger can give big, nutty wines. His
peachy/nutty 1989 Auslese was delicious. Alphart
makes some red wines from both Blauer Portugieser and Zweigelt. The Zweigelt is the best as he
knows how to keep this heavy cropper down to a
sensible 35 hl/ha to concentrate all the grape's
cherry flavours.

Johann Stadlmann has a popular *Buschenschank* on the main street of Traiskirchen. Like

Gumpoldskirchen. The hills around the touristy village are the pays d'élection *for the Zierflandler and Rotgipfler grapes.*

Alphart he contrives to make a classy Rhine Riesling in a region not generally noted for this variety. He is best known for his traditional wines, however, made from the Rotgipfler and Zierfandler grapes. As ever, it is a pity that the Austrians are so impatient to drink their wines, as neither of these Südbahn standbys shows its best until it has been in bottle for a few years. Stadlmann's 1989 Rotgipfler Spätlese was just beginning to show the richness of its brown bread and peaches character when I tried it in 1991, while the Zierfandler Beerenauslese still needed time. Stadlmann made a superb *Ausbruch* in 1990 which, with time (if it survives), could live to match the wonderful Zierfandler Trockenbeeren-auslese he made in 1973.

Further down the main street of Traiskirchen, on the same side of the road is the Schafler *Buschenschank*. Here young **Andreas Schafler** has taken over the winemaking and is pushing aside a certain amount of the old style of the Südbahn in favour of new grapes and more modern vinification techniques. He is most proud of his Chardonnay, half of which he ferments in new oak barrels and then houses in large oak tuns to avoid an excessive oaky taste getting into the wine. Some *Prädikat* wines are made in good years, such as 1990, and here even the Rotgipfler is used to effect, producing creamy, pineappley flavours. Neuburger is once

again the Schafler's main variety, although here the wines are quite angular compared to most. Schafler makes an excellent Traminer wine most years and a red Südbahn Cuvée from St-Laurent and Zweigelt grapes.

Since before Franz Schams' time, the southern part of the Thermenregion has been better known for its red wines than its whites (*see p 23*). The principal grape variety for red wines is the high-yielding and generally undistinguished Blauer Portugieser, which was the mainstay of the 'Vöslauer' red wine of so many a Viennese *Beisl*. There is a story (and not a particularly trustworthy one) that the Blauer Portugieser was brought back from Portugal to Austria by an Austrian diplomat called Graf Fries at the beginning of the last century. Graf Fries is therefore the name of the best Blauer Portugieser produced by **Johann Gisperg** in the village of Teesdorf.

The key to the success of red wines here lies in the soils of Teesdorf and Tattendorf: they are in the main gravelly or stoney, providing an ideally poor earth for quality red-wine vines. Blauer Portugieser is not often included in that category, but Gisperg knows how to deal with it: his lightest wines are made in a Beaujolais style – ideal for summer picnics – while another *cuvée* is reserved for more extractive wines. The best Blauer Portugieser goes into Graf Fries. Gisperg makes other red wines: quite splendid St-Laurents and Zweigelts and a remarkable Blauburgunder Spätlese with really earthy, burgundian character.

Another man noted for his ability to handle the tricky Burgundian grape is **Christian Fischer** in Sooss, who made excellent Blauburgunders in 1989, 1988 and 1985. Fischer is also one of the best makers of St-Laurent in Austria, producing really dense, fruity wines. Fischer's ability to handle red wine grapes makes him a specialist of both Zweigelt and Blauer Portugieser. In 1989 he harvested his first Cabernet Sauvignon; there is every reason to believe that he will succeed there too.

Also in Sooss is the Grabner-Schierer *Buschenschank*. The wines are now made by **Sepp Schierer** who married into the Grabner family in the 1970s. Schierer makes a quite remarkable Blauer Portugieser which seems to defy all the usual criticisms levelled at the grape; for a start it is long, and packed with good, dense, raspberry and cherry fruit. Another wine to look out for is his St-Laurent which has lashings of strawberry aromas. In his time Sepp Schierer has made some wonderfully concentrated Blauburgunders, but in recent years

he has taken to putting the wines in 100 percent new Limousin and Allier oak. I fear this is too much for the poor wine. Watch out, though, for a successful Cabernet Sauvignon from this house; it is one of the few in Austria made from old vines.

One of the men most highly praised for his Cabernet Sauvignon wines in modern Austria is **Johann Reinisch** of the Johanneshof in Tattendorf. More than 70 percent of Reinisch's wines are red and nearly 30 percent of the vineyard is planted with Cabernet Sauvignon, Cabernet Franc and Merlot. Reinisch has spent some time at Clos du Val in California and he is clearer than most new-wave Austrian winemakers about the style he wants to achieve. He makes a convincingly New World-style, *barrique*-fermented Chardonnay; a decent Blauburgunder, which lacks something of the earthy 'breed' I associate with burgundy; and his pride and joy, the Cabernet/Merlot blend.

Reinisch does not limit himself to international styles (although he does manage to vinify some of his Blauer Portugieser as a 'sherry' by using a sort of *solera* system!) and he makes a very successful blend of Weissburgunder and Welschriesling as well as a surprisingly good oak-aged Neuburger.

Harvesting the grapes in Tattendorf. Tattendorf's gravelly soils make it ideal for red wine production.

BURGENLAND

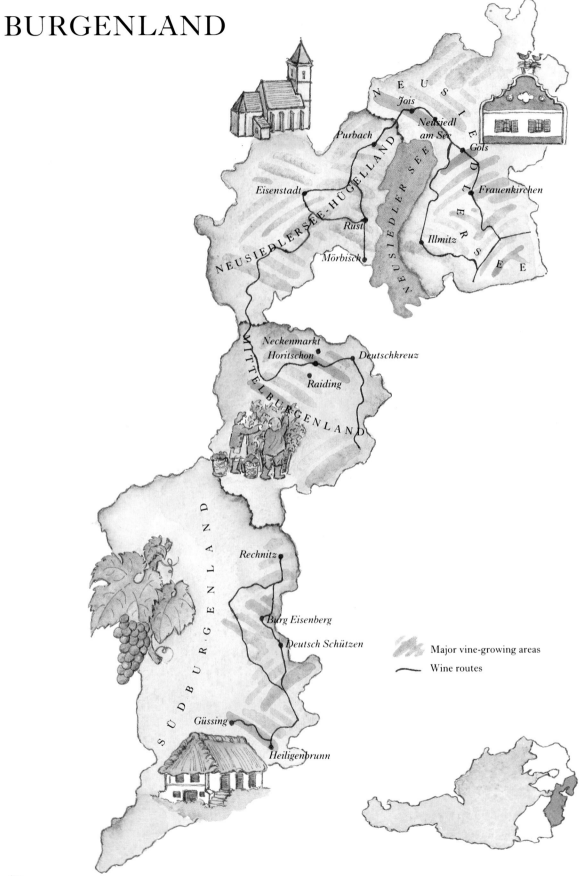

NEUSIEDLERSEE

Jois

Neusiedl
am See

Purbach

Gols

Eisenstadt

Frauenkirchen

NEUSIEDLERSEE-HÜGELLAND

Rust

NEUSIEDLER SEE

Illmitz

Mörbisch

Neckenmarkt
Horitschon

Deutschkreuz

MITTELBURGENLAND

Raiding

SÜDBURGENLAND

Rechnitz

Burg Eisenberg

Deutsch Schützen

Major vine-growing areas

Wine routes

Güssing

Heiligenbrunn

NEUSIEDLERSEE-HÜGELLAND

In the wider world the mention of the Neusiedlersee conjures up images of storks and very sweet wines. The storks are certainly there (in the summer months) and so are the sweet wines, but the latter are very largely confined to a thin strip of land which lies between the lakeside road and the water itself. If you cross to the other side of the road, the benevolent fungus *Botrytis cinerea*, vital for the creation of these wines, occurs in quantity only two years in ten and here the wines are generally dry reds and dry whites.

Most wine lovers would be astonished to learn of the variety of wine styles now being made on the shores of the shallow Neusiedlersee. Here are not just some of the most interesting Cabernets, Pinot Noirs, Chardonnays and Sauvignon Blancs to emerge from the new Austria, but also other grape varieties one would hardly dream of finding here: Syrah, Nebbiolo, Sangiovese. They are all grown and much more besides.

At first sight Rust would seem to be at the centre of traditional thinking as far as Neusiedlersee-Hügelland is concerned; but once you have scratched the surface you will see that this is far from being the case. There are only a handful of full-time growers in the old free city and the rest tend to bottle a little sweet wine and take the rest of their grapes to the Weinkellerei Burgenland up the road. Some of these small growers' *Beerenauslesen* and *Trockenbeerenauslesen* will be delicious; others less good – it is a small risk.

Among the professional growers you will find not only a very high standard of winemaking, but also a very keen awareness of the history and traditions of the city and of one of the world's greatest dessert wines which was and is made here: I am speaking, of course, of *Ausbruch*.

The first stop for an *Ausbruch* fanatic is **Robert Wenzel**, who occupies a large and ancient house down by the lake. It is filled with artefacts pertaining to his love for the old Habsburg monarchy. Rumour has it that Wenzel speaks as many languages as the devil. I cannot substantiate this, but I will say that he speaks a wonderfully mellifluous and beautifully articulated German.

The two traditional varieties here in Rust are the Furmint and the Gelber Muskateller, which is sometimes given the Hungarian name of Muscat Lunel. The Furmint has a ferocious acidity, which

Above: A stork's nest.
Left: Rust, home of Ausbruch.

is its chief advantage in nobly rotten wines. Vinified dry, as it sometimes is with Wenzel, it can be a rather searing, appley wine. The Gelber Muskateller is rather nicer in this raw state as there is more spice and more aroma. At higher *Prädikat* levels, Wenzel tends to blend grapes: a Beerenauslese 1990 was made from Furmint, Muskateller and Müller-Thurgau, putting me in mind of pineapple with cream cheese.

With more than three centuries of Wenzel wine-making in the same house in Rust and a father somewhere in the building rumoured to be as much as 100 years old, Robert Wenzel knows a thing or two about *Ausbruch* and how it should be made. In former times *Ausbruch* wines spent longer in cask than they do today, anything up to ten years. Furthermore, the Rusters did not get sufficient *Botrytis* to make an *Ausbruch* wine every year: about one in two was the average.

The key problem for *Ausbruch*-makers is to keep the fermentation going when there is so much sugar and so little liquid in the musts. In classic *Ausbruch* the winemaker added fresh, non *Botrytis*-affected, grapes or fresh must. The results were more 'vinous' than the German *Trockenbeerenauslese* and, with such a long time in cask, there was often a touch of *rancio*, or an oxidised, almost sherryish character to the wines.

We tasted a fresh Ausbruch 1990 from the cask which had not had time to assume this style. A 1984 Ruländer Ausbruch, however, had been bottled after four years in cask; here too were *rancio*-like flavours: orange, tobacco and dried herbs.

Anyone who wants a demonstration of what *Ausbruch* is about should pay a call on **Peter Schandl**, a big, warm fellow, not unlike the late James Robertson-Justice in appearance. Schandl is an excellent teacher: Tokay *Ausbruch*, he explains, was made by adding buckets full of *Trockenbeeren* to the must. In Rust it was otherwise: fresh grapes were added instead to the *Trockenbeeren*, this had the advantage of making the wines of Rust more 'elegant' than those of Tokay. Without a system of this sort the berries simply will not ferment. "*Ausbruch*", says Schandl, "has nothing *whatsoever* to do with *Trockenbeerenauslese*."

Patting a full sized papier-mâché dummy called Leopold on the head ("Women occasionally

embrace him!" says Schandl), Schandl took me into his drawing room. Here he proceeded to show me the difference between the two styles. He still makes *Trockenbeerenauslese* when the fermentation goes too quickly. Then the winey character of the *Ausbruch* disappears and it makes a sort of 'concentrate' which is typically *Trockenbeerenauslese*. He showed me a wine and asked me what I thought: it seemed pretty good to me. "It has 27° KMW and I could call it an *Ausbruch*, but for me it hasn't got the character." He had decided to downgrade it to *Beerenauslese*. Another *Ausbruch*-strength *Beerenauslese* followed, this time a Neuburger. This could have been an *Ausbruch* too with 27.5° KMW, he told me, dismissing the wine. Then he brought out a 1989 Ruländer and I began to see what he

indeed a 'concentrate': lovely in itself, but less of a pleasant drinking experience than the Ausbruch.

Schandl began to talk about worms: worms make the *Prädikat* wines in these parts. "First comes the hay-worm, in May and June, this attacks the flowers; then comes the sour-worm, the son of the hay-worm. The sour-worm drills into the infant bunches to make them sour. The third generation is the sweet-worm which penetrates the skins of the grapes in September allowing *Botrytis* to creep in: only the sweet-worm is benign."

It would be wrong to leave Schandl without mentioning his other wines. Schandl has 15 hectares and only a few of these are dedicated to *Prädikat*-style varieties. Schandl makes big Weissburgunders benefiting from the warmth of the soil in Rust and a Rhine Riesling with almond and lime aromas, which is considered one of the best in the region. He has a Cabernet Sauvignon/Cabernet Franc/Merlot blend which is good and solid and for once not herbaceous! He also has old Blauburgunder vines planted by his father; these have good, chunky fruit. The 1986 was his greatest recent success with this grape: full of chocolate and raspberry fruit and quite delicious.

Next door to Schandl, **Bruno Landauer** is also specialising in sweet wines. Until recently Landauer used to sell off a large part of the production of his and his wife's 18-hectare vineyard to the cooperative. This allowed him to undertake some vital work in the cellars and bring in some new equipment. Around his smart new tasting room Landauer has suspended pictures of bunches of grapes in various stages of infection by *Botrytis*. It is not a pretty sight: the totally rotten Zweigelt put me in mind of some diseased human organ displayed in a medical museum. One wonders who it was who first had the courage to try these grapes and work out that they could make superb wine.

Landauer has a lot of Müller-Thurgau, which is not a grape which excites a passion in me; but I liked his white pepper and raspberries-scented Blaufränkisch 1990. The good, sweet wines begin with a 1990 Neuburger Spätlese with a nice creamy, nutty character and a couple of Gewürz-

meant. This was indeed more vinous: pumpernickel tastes merged with classic *Botrytis* flavours; it was more like a Sauternes than a *Trockenbeerenauslese. This* was *Ausbruch.*

Schandl is informative about grapes too, "without *Botrytis*, Furmint is without interest; it is a mass-producer." Schandl thinks that people simply had better ideas in the wake of phylloxera and did not replant. On the other hand he is forced to admit that *he* has planted Furmint recently, and not only Furmint, but Gelber Muskateller. Schandl went off to fetch an Ausbruch Ruländer from 1981, the last great sweet wine year, so that he could compare it to a 1981 Trockenbeerenauslese Ruländer. The Ausbruch was full of ripe, coffee-scented fruit; the Trockenbeerenauslese was traminers; a 1990 Spätlese which was perhaps a mite too sweet and a 1989 Auslese which was rather better structured. Walnuts dominated the Weissburgunder Auslese 1987.

Landauer's classic, high-alcohol (14–15°) Welschriesling Ausbruch was elected to the Salon. It is a delicious wine with lashings of apricot and plum fruit. His *Eisweine* are less classic, as he believes that it is possible to make them with slightly rotten grapes. I am afraid that I do not agree and was uncomfortable with the mushroomy aromas in his 1988 Welschriesling Eiswein. The 1989 Goldburger Eiswein, however, was another kettle of fish: Landauer had put this wine (made from totally healthy grapes) into new oak, which made it taste of toffee bananas. New oak had also been successfully used on the 1989 Welschriesling Ausbruch. Landauer makes a little brandy, which is marketed under the name of Rustiak!

Heidi Schröck is one of a small band of female Austrian winemakers. She makes wines of all styles from dry whites, to reds and *Ausbrüche*. I was much taken with her dry (but powerful) 1990 Ruländer with its concentrated, radishy fruit. The 1990 Zweigelt is a classic with its cherry aromas, while a 1986 Blaufränkisch had some nice, dense coffee notes. Like Wenzel, Heidi makes her *Ausbruch* from a wide palette of grapes, fermenting wines like the 1990 to a powerful 15.5°. We finished our tasting with two wines made by Heidi's father: a 1967 Sauvignon Blanc Ausbruch with lots of honey and toffee tastes; and the wine which Herr Schröck

describes as "The best wine I have ever made", a 1973 Welschriesling labelled Trockenbeerenauslese, but in reality an *Ausbruch*. The fact that it is an *Ausbruch* is evident from the strength, 13.4°, and its vinous qualities. It was a superb glass with a complex palate of sweet rice, pineapple, mangoes and quinces.

The mislabelling of Herr Schröck's wine pinpoints one of the reasons why *Ausbruch* succumbed for a large part of this century. With West Germany as the major foreign customer, growers were anxious to make wines which would be easily recognisable to Germans raised on the rare *Prädikat* wines of the Rhine and Mosel. Some Rusters, like **Hans Holler** at the Elfenhof, still lead far more on the German styles than the native Rust ones. Holler makes some sweet red wines which I do not get along with, but I like his white *Prädikat* wines: a fat, luscious 1981 Weissburgunder Auslese; a golden, peachy 1979 Ruländer Beerenauslese and a

Above: Heidi Schröck in her cellar in Rust.

proper Ausbruch 1981 made from Gewürztra-miner grapes which was bottled after ten years in cask! This wine was brimming with coffee, choco-late and plum flavours. Another *Ausbruch*, this time a 1976 Ruländer, put me in mind of those lovely Manon chocolates you buy in Brussels: all coffee and cream. The last of these wonderful bottles was a 1969 Weissburgunder Trockenbeerenauslese, 500 bottles of which Holler found hidden recently behind a cask. This was very much a *Trockenbeeren-auslese*: a concentration of caramelly fruit.

The Feiler-Artinger house is another Renais-sance building in the street leading down to the lake. It is **Frau Feiler** (whose brother is the mayor of Rust) who generally deals with the wine side of things, and not her husband, Hans. In the 20 hectares of vineyard the Feiler-Artingers make a wide variety of wines, including a chunky Blau-fränkisch. Some of this they put into new oak, which I think mars the lovely spicy, plum and cherry fruit. Look out for a 1989 Gewürztraminer Spätlese with a bouquet of yellow roses, and a Welschriesling Auslese which smelled of jelly babies. The Feilers do not make any of the German *Prädikat* styles and concentrate on *Ausbruch*: of which there was a fine 1988 Weissburgunder and an even better Pinot Cuvée (Ruländer and Weissbur-gunder) of the same year. Much of the charm of the latter comes from the banana-toffee aromas sup-plied by new oak, but here it does not offend me as the fruit is so rich that it marries up perfectly.

Both the Triebaumer brothers are more famous for their red wines than they are for their *Ausbrüche*; which is not to say they do not make them: they do, and some of the best in Rust. **Ernst Triebaumer** took me out to see his vineyards, which lie dotted over the commune. His *Ausbruch* vineyards are down by the lake where he has recently planted proper Gelber (as opposed to Grüner) Furmint. The yellow Furmint has smaller berries than the

Centre: Big tuns in Hans Feiler's old cellars. The Feiler-Artinger domaine is noted for Ausbruch *and* Blaufränkisch *wines.*
Left: The Renaissance courtyard of the Feiler-Artinger house; this is one of several superb buildings in the street leading down to the lake.

green variety, which a century ago were called *Jungfernbeeren* (virgin berries). The Gelber Furmint has the advantage of being more resistant to disease than the Grüner. Recently as many as six Rusters have replanted the old Furmint; Triebaumer thinks the figure will increase to three dozen over the next few years.

Across the road, away from the *Botrytis*, Triebaumer has T-grafted his Müller-Thurgau vines to Cabernet Sauvignon and Nebbiolo. Elsewhere he showed me Merlot and Sauvignon Blanc grapes, the latter already shrivelling up with noble rot; some tiny plots of Sangiovese, Dolcetto and Gamay and then finally his Blaufränkisch vines, on which his fame is chiefly based.

Ernst Triebaumer is an excellent winemaker who makes a great many superb wines; far too many to describe here. His 1990 Sauvignon is notable for its convincing catty flavours and his Gewürztraminer Auslese Trocken 1990 would rival anything from Alsace. Triebaumer makes a plump, international-style Chardonnay which is fermented in new oak. Then comes *Ausbruch*. Triebaumer's method is to add 30–40 percent of fresh grapes to the *Trockenbeeren* and then stamp the must with his bare feet. He uses different white grapes for this. In 1989 he made a delicious wine marred only by a slightly hot finish from the alcohol (it fermented up to 17.7 percent!). In some years Triebaumer has made *Trockenbeerenauslese*, but only when that has proved the easiest option.

Ernst Triebaumer's best reds come from the Blaufränkisch vineyards. A simple Qualitätswein 1990 was as good as many top Blaufränkisch wines from other estates, with that typical white-pepper-and-raspberries aroma. From Ried Gmärk came another 1990 with more interesting cherry notes. The 1989 from Ried Oberer Wald had a little new oak, but it was well integrated into the cherry/raspberry fruit. The very best was the 1989 Ried Mariental, with its medley of toffee, raspberry, violet and fresh fig flavours.

Ernst's brother, **Paul Triebaumer**, lives on the other side of Rust. Like Ernst he is a tireless experimenter who has produced wonderful things in the ten years since he stopped taking his grapes to the Weinkellerei Burgenland. One of these is his *Keltenwein*: a 'Celtic' wine inspired by the disco-very by some local archaeologists of grape pips attesting to the use of noble grape varieties in Burgenland long before the arrival of the Romans (*see p* 10). It is a perfectly natural Welschriesling, bottled in beer bottles with a cork and a crown cap. As there is no sulphur, the wine oxidises rapidly on opening.

Like his brother, Paul Triebaumer has some Chardonnay. Here I prefer the more angular, unoaked version to that which goes into Allier and Nevers oak. Triebaumer makes some delicious *Prädikat* wines from Neuburger, such as his lavender-scented, nutty 1990 Spätlese. Gewürztraminer is another star here: a particular favourite of Frau Triebaumer. The 1990 Auslese has enchanting yellow rose and banana aromas while a 1980 Eiswein was like honey and peaches.

Paul Triebaumer also has strong views when it comes to Ruster *Ausbruch*: "the only truly Austrian *Prädikat appellation*". He too has planted Gelber Furmint but is alarmed by its acidity, which can creep up to 22 g/l. He wants, therefore, to put the wine through malolactic fermentation to tame it a little. *Ausbruch*, according to Paul Triebaumer, must be high in alcohol and spend at best three or more years in cask: "it is nothing in the least like *Trockenbeerenauslese*." He also points out that the old term *klibern* described grapes which had not entirely shrivelled, so that there remained a little moisture to help the fermentation. *Trockenbeerenauslese* is also impossible with 100 percent nobly rotten fruit – it will not ferment. Like his brother he treads the grapes with his feet.

As he spoke he brought out a 1981 Weissburgunder Ausbruch from the last superlative *Botrytis* year. This spent three years in oak, giving it a coffee-bean character to enhance the apricot and peach fruit. This will be replaced by a 1989 Neuburger Ausbruch, which spent two years in cask with the same fresh, ripe apricot aromas. A 1981 Neuburger Trockenbeerenauslese was no disappointment either.

Like his brother, Paul Triebaumer is famous for his reds. He is the only man in Austria so far to plant half an hectare of Syrah. Sadly, the vines were not yet in production, but I was able to try a range of wonderful Blaufränkisch wines, such as the 1990 from Ried Pfarrergmärk or the violet, blackberry-

Vineyards in Oggau, the next village up from Rust.

and cherry-scented 1989 from Ried Pandkräften. Another hot tip is the quality of Blauburgunders, of which both the 1989 and 1988 had good, earthy breed. Lastly, I tried Austria's first-ever Nebbiolo. This was an exciting wine with lots of cherry and mulberry aromas: one to watch.

The Haus Marienberg in Oggau is owned by **Wilhelm Mad** and his family. Despite any contrary impression you might have from his name, he is a perfectly reasonable man. For a start, he has recently completely rethought his planting technique, abandoning the ubiquitous *Hochkultur* for *Vertico* planting (a term which describes itself). He has also made his vines denser to stimulate competition in the vineyard. The Mad vineyards are organic; as much as possible sprays have been eliminated and he tries to get his neighbours to do the same. Yields are low: 40 hl/ha for whites and 35 hl/ha for reds; this he ensures by means of a rigorous *vendange verte*. Grapes are picked in five stages. Firstly, Blaufränkisch, Zweigelt and St-Laurent for his rosé; secondly, Rhine Riesling;

thirdly, Weissburgunder; fourthly, overripe grapes such as Chardonnay and the big reds; finally, *Prädikat* wines.

In his vineyards not far from the Neusiedlersee, Mad can benefit from the warmth of the soil to ensure that his grapes achieve just the degree of ripeness he wants. This helps enormously to give that plump style that he is looking for in his Chardonnay from Ried Pratschkräfte, for example, which attains an easy *Auslese* level (and is of course vinified bone-dry). In Ried Haide Mad makes a good, concentrated Zweigelt from low yields. Blauburgunder is another success here, even if it has lost something of the force, say, of Schandl's and the finesse of Paul Triebaumer's. His best red is probably his own favourite: the St-Laurent from Ried Waidacker with its light blackcurrant fruit. St-Laurent enters the *cuvée* with Blauburgunder and Blaufränkisch with its nice mulberry and plum character (in Austria *cuvée* is the term used to describe a blend of different grape varieties). The *cuvée* is aged in 50 percent new Allier oak. Haus Marienberg does not really specialise in *Prädikat* wines, but he makes some extremely good ones from time to time. In general Mad tries to make an *Eiswein* from some Goldburger grapes which he keeps for that purpose.

In the low hills just above Oggau is the village of Schützen am Gebirge which is the home of **Engelbert Prieler**. On the heavy loam soils this far from the lake, the chances of *Botrytis* are slight. In general, Prieler's wines are dry. He also specialises in brandies, putting the spirits into what he calls *Damenflaschen*, a term apparently derived from the very phallic shape of the bottles. As far as white wines are concerned, the lion's share is Weissburgunder, although Prieler has a very good reputation for his Welschriesling; this is clean and steely, a classic *Reparaturwein*, capable of bringing the palate back to life after cloying food or sweet wines.

Prieler made classic, nutty Weissburgunder in the vintages from 1987–90, and put some of the 1990 vintage into new oak, with interesting results. My favourite in this impressive series would be the 1988, in which a small amount of *Botrytis* gave the wine a rather more toasty character. Prieler is also a believer in St-Laurent, Austria's most fickle red wine variety. His 1990 was lovely with its raspberry/strawberry fruit; the 1988 seemed a mite jammy on the nose but the palate was nicely structured. His Blaufränkisch wines win competitions year in year out; both the 1989 and the 1990 were marked by a strong peppery character which

The excellent Taubenkobel in Schützen am Gebirge.

Prieler puts down to the soil. He uses some new oak for these wines, but in general it is well integrated and not used as a flavour in itself. The last red wine he markets is his *cuvée*, in which the proportion of Cabernet Sauvignon has been staggering up by the year. His Cabernet is big and it tends to swamp the Blaufränkisch. A Cabernet/Merlot blend is billed.

Mention should be made of the schnapps in the famous *Damenflaschen*. A Muskat Ottonel schnapps is housed in Acacia oak and, like the Traminer, it keeps its grape character. Prieler makes brandy in Limousin casks from Bouvier or Grüner Veltliner. The Grüner Veltliner is enchantingly smoky. A Weissburgunder grappa, aged in small casks, has a pleasant floral character.

Mörbisch is on the other side of Rust, a lakeside village famous for its music festival and its floral courtyards. The mayor of Mörbisch is **Franz Schindler**, who has some very old Blaufränkisch vines as well as some rather younger Cabernet. Schindler has gone overboard on oak. This sometimes leads to strange results with the wine, which is not always able to take prolonged periods in small oak casks. Personally, I should be happy with the straight, plums-and-spice wine he made in 1990, but when you tell Schindler you like this kind of thing, his eyes light up and he tells you that he intends to imprison it in small oak for a further 18 months. Some Blaufränkisch is cut with Cabernet and this seems able to take the barrel treatment better. His best wines are the Cuvée d'Or, which are pure Blaufränkisch. The oak gives them a slightly oxidised character, but this is not always disagreeable. Many growers in Mörbisch make an *Opernball* white wine from Welschriesling. It should be fresh and neutral: Welschriesling is naturally ideal for this.

Smack on the Hungarian frontier in Zagersdorf is the home of **Franz and Rosi Schuster**. The wines are signed Rosi Schuster, but both husband and wife make them. Franz also teaches winemaking at the wine school in Eisenstadt. The Schuster wines are impressive; here things seem to be a little more reasoned than they are with some of the winemakers on the shores of the lake. An unusual soil gives some interesting results too. Schuster believes that wine needs heat (he heats the musts before fermentation) and movement (ie racking).

There are three top wines from the estate: a straight Blaufränkisch called Classique; a Blaufränkisch which goes into small oak; and CMB: a blend of Cabernet, Merlot and Blaufränkisch.

The Classique has some nice dusty raspberry flavours, which in the now mature 1986 have evolved into a bouquet of violets and herbs. As they get older they get figgy, as was borne out by both the 1983 and the 1981. The CMB sometimes has a nice whiff of dill, especially the 1989 vintage.

A few kilometres to the southwest is Pöttelsdorf, another village with a preponderance of red wine. Like quite a number of villages in Burgenland, Pöttelsdorf is Protestant. Its people were formerly protected from the Catholic court in Vienna by virtue of the fact that they belonged to the crown of Hungary and were guaranteed by ancient laws. I imagine that Otto von Bismarck knew this much when he took a shine to the wine of Pöttelsdorf after the Battle of Königgrätz in 1866. Bismarck was served it at a meal one night and from that moment on the anti-Catholic Iron Chancellor placed regular orders with a wine merchant in Eisenstadt. The wines have been associated with Bismarck ever since. They are now even served to passengers on Austrian trains and railways, which is ironic in a way: after all, Bismarck did his bit to hasten the end of Austria's claims to world power.

Now all the wines are called Fürst Bismarck and most are made from Blaufränkisch. The cellar operates as a cooperative for local growers; white wine grapes have to be taken to Rust to the cooperative there. There are 200 hectares of Blaufränkisch on the slopes and plains of Pöttelsdorf (plenty to provide for even the gargantuan appetites of a Bismarck). Four main wines are produced: straight Fürst Bismarck; a Fass 2 for the best selection; a *barrique* wine; and Bankett, a wine left five months on its *marc* before being pressed and bottled. Of the four I must say that I think the best value is the cheapest: straight Fürst Bismarck with its pleasant white-pepper-and-raspberry fruit. Unless it is in the hands of a real master, Blaufränkisch is sometimes a little short, but this is the only real drawback of this grape.

The capital of Burgenland is the old city of Eisenstadt, with its old churches, fine local museum and usual Austrian array of convents and monasteries. The order of the **Barmherzigen Brüder** actually runs the main hospital in the free city; but, like most Austrian religious foundations, the Barmherzigen Brüder have a few vines as well.

The brothers run a very clean cellar and have allowed their winemaker a large budget to invest in new equipment and French oak barrels. There are some good Welschrieslings, not the fashionable

Vineyards near Eisenstadt. The free city was long the residence of the Esterhazy family, the patrons of Haydn.

The vineyards on the Leitha hills near Eistenstadt.

angular wines, but fatter brews which are often chaptalised to round off the fruit. The Blaufränkisch wines fall into three types: a straight large oak style; a small oak wine (*barrique*); and Haydn (he worked for the Esterházys in their vast palace round the corner), the best traditional Blaufränkisch. For me the best of the 'normal' wines were the 1990 and the 1989 with their slightly leathery, blackberry and raspberry fruit. My favourite *barrique* wines were the 1989 and the 1987; the latter in particular had a classy violet note. Haydn seemed at its most melodious in the 1990 vintage. The Barmherzigen Brüder also make a nice Müller-Thurgau and a Welschriesling brandy which puts some of the Limousin oak to a more fitting use.

Near Eisenstadt is the village of Grosshöflein which possesses a collection of famous winemakers. Chief among these is **Anton Kollwentz** at the Römerhof. Kollwentz has been one of Austrian wines' greatest innovators over the past two decades, and his palate is much in demand from the many Austrian wine reviews.

Kollwentz presides over some very up-to-date equipment in his cellars, and a collection of wines which he has acquired from every wine-producing country in the world. It is hard to catch him out here: to my questions about wines from England and what was East Germany he was able to put his hands instantly on appropriate samples.

Kollwentz is quite a commercial operation: he gives the modern Austrian wine-snob precisely what he wants. Whites are angular and clean; reds are often given new oak flavours. From the whites I liked his grassy Sauvignon Blanc and a delicious 1989 Welschriesling Eiswein. With the reds I often found myself edging round the wine in the hope of penetrating the fruit through the oak flavouring. For this reason, perhaps, I appreciated a simple 1990 Zweigelt and two Blaufränkisch wines from the same vintage; one of which was earmarked for bottling and the other which had been condemned to 18 months in oak. The 1989s showed the same problem: the unoaked wine I liked unreservedly, the oaked wine (more expensive too) seemed coated with oak flavours which were not really part of the wine. This oaking policy works best with Cabernet, and Kollwentz's experiments with this grape are some of the earliest and the best. He got nice, figgy, blackcurrant notes on his 1989 and 1986 and a 1983 had a pleasant smoky tone.

Rudolf Wagentristl of Grosshöflein has come to the fore rather more recently than Kollwentz, but with the string of accolades he has received from the national wine press he is catching up quickly. Again, his is basically a red-wine house, exploiting the chalk and primary rock soils of the Leitha hills; but he is capable of making a very seductive dry Muskat-Ottonel and he usually brings off an *Eiswein* like the huge, mango-scented 1983 Neuburger. Wagentristl has a very good Blauburgunder and his 1986 justified a prize from *Falstaff* magazine. I must confess that in this

instance I was rather more impressed by an exemplary series of Zweigelts with great flavour in their cherry, raspberry, violet and chocolate fruit. Look out also for Wagentristl's Blaufränkisch wines.

Josef Leberl is another name to conjure with. He is a warm, friendly man who has been making wine in Grosshöflein for ten years and has recently invested prodigious sums in his cellar to acquire the latest technology. Leberl is another Austrian bitten by the Cabernet bug. In his cellars are rows of barrels from the Austrian firm of Schneckenleitner (they were the ones who convinced everybody to put their wine in Limousin oak; in France this is generally thought too coarse for wine and is reserved for Cognac). One whole row is surveyed by the *Kellerkatze*. Traditionally this wooden effigy of a cat sits on the estate's best barrel; *chez* Leberl it is the Cabernet Sauvignon which the cat safeguards.

Leberl is a meticulous man and this is evident in his wines. "My favourite work is pruning", he told me, which, given the temperature here in January, must count as a perversion. Among his whites there is a good Sauvignon Blanc which is sold to the Drei Husaren restaurant in Vienna. The 1989 had big, pease-pudding flavours. With a Purbach lawyer called **Hans Bichler**, Leberl makes an oak-aged Ruländer with attractive, spicy, radishy notes. The Sauvignon Blanc occasionally reappears as a *Prädikat* wine with a 1988 Beerenauslese showing a lovely mushrooms and oranges aroma. Leberl can also do good things with Scheurebe, getting grapefruit flavours on his delicious 1989 Eiswein.

Leberl makes tight, long-lasting reds. His Zweigelts vie with Wagentristl's for concentration in their cherry fruitiness. The Blaufränkisch gets classic white-pepper-and-raspberry fruit which Leberl coats with a little oak. The 1989 is sullen now, but with time the wine absorbs these oaky flavours, as was borne out by the 1985. Then there is his pride and joy (at twice the price of either Blaufränkisch or Zweigelt): Cabernet Sauvignon. This gets 100 percent new oak. The wines have plenty of tannins and seem well balanced; time will tell whether the 1989 or the 1990 had enough fruit to support such a heavy oaking.

The harvest in a wide-spaced modern vineyard in Burgenland.

NEUSIEDLERSEE

The second of Burgenland's four *appellations* divides into two stylistic zones. The first of these centres on the 'wine village' of Gols in the north of the region. Here the wines are most likely to be sturdy reds and dry whites. To the south is the Seewinkel (literally Lake Corner) on the Hungarian border. Here a succession of small pools, ponds and lakes, with evocative names like the Oberer Stinkensee and the Unterer Stinkensee, produce a permanently damp climate which ensures constant *Botrytis*. Like it or not, in the Seewinkel *Botrytis* is likely to attack just about everything, even, I have heard it asserted, the growers themselves.

The largely protestant town of Gols is an ugly place: a swollen village filled with drab facades; yet Gols ranks with Langenlois as Austria's greatest wine-producing commune and some of the wine made here can rank with the best in Europe. One Golser with a supra-national reputation is **Georg Stiegelmar** who runs a smallish domaine with his well-travelled son **Axel**. The Steigelmars are addicted to international competitions, and for good reason: they have the knack of winning, and if they do not they get placed pretty near the top.

The Stiegelmars spread themselves about a bit; they have a nice old cellar in the *Kellergasse* for their reds and another for the whites and in the centre of Gols they also have a *Buschenschank*. The Stiegelmars' best whites are their Weissburgunders, Chardonnays and Gewürztraminers. The Weissburgunders benefit considerably from bottle-age

when they develop some attractive gooseberry/rhubarb character. Sometimes they make a Prädikat Weissburgunder as in the 1976 Trockenbeerenauslese with its wood-smoke and apricot aromas. The Stiegelmars have adopted a rather odd practice of putting pebbles in the bottoms of these old bottles. This is a reference to the habit in older times of placing pebbles in casks after you had drawn off a glass in order to prevent the level from falling and the wine from oxidising. However, wine should not oxidise in a bottle and most buyers must

Stalagtites in the cellars of Georg Stiegelmar in Gols.

be more than perplexed to find that their precious flasks contain *Stein* rather than *Weinstein*.

The Stiegelmars are immensely proud of the Chardonnay they make in an international, oaky style. Once or twice they have made a sweet wine which I do not take to. My favourite among their whites was an Alsace-style dry Auslese Gewürztraminer 1989 with its spicy lemon-peel character.

The Stiegelmars have planted Cabernet Sauvignon, but I have tasted only two infant wines in cask and I shall defer judgement until the wine begins to

develop some recognisable features. One of their best reds is the St-Laurent with its chunky strawberry flavours. This was particularly successful in 1989 when there was more of a chocolate and morello cherry character. The Stiegelmar Blauburgunder 1987 was the first Austrian red wine I ever drank and I was quite bowled over by its quality; I am still fond of it, and the 1985 which I have tasted more recently. The 1986 is slightly leaner and not so characteristic of the grape. Finally, there is the St-Georg *cuvée* made up of Zweigelt, St-Laurent and Blauburgunder. This is generally a big, hunky wine.

Also in Gols are the vineyards of **Erich Heinrich** and his son **Gernot**. The Heinrichs specialise in Weissburgunder for their whites, making very individual, spicy wines and every now and then a dry *Spätlese*. Other whites include a rare Roter Riesling, from a clonal mutation of the Rhine Riesling (the 1990 had a lime and apples character) and a good dry Auslese Neuburger from the Ried Goldberg which tasted of baked apples. There are some good, characterful St-Laurents with aromas of brown sugar and nuts, and deep-coloured Zweigelts, some of which Heinrich puts into Styrian, Manhartsberg or Allier oak.

The current cynosure in Gols is **Hans Nittnaus** who makes some of the most tannic reds in Austria. His popularity has proved a double-edged sword now that he has no more wine to sell and none to apportion to the export market that he once dreamed of breaking into. The immense tannins he gets on his wines can be a problem too, as was demonstrated by a tragi-comic story he told me in his cellar: he had sent a consignment of his big, brooding 1989 Blaufränkisch to a well-known Vienna restaurant, but the restaurant later returned most of the bottles and demanded they be credited for the amount. The reason: the wine had been aged in oak *barriques* but did not taste of new oak, and they did not think they could sell them at the price. This has something important to say about the shallow folly of the present Austrian barrel cult; barrel flavourings in wine are at best a happy accident, at worst fraud.

Gols in the Seewinkel, the most productive wine village in Austria, famed for its deep red wines and sweet whites.

As usual, Nittnaus does not confine his attentions to one wine and he makes a number of whites. His Sauvignon Blanc has a racy asparagus flavour and he makes a convincing Rhine Riesling from his vineyard in the Ried Altenberg. A 1988 Chardonnay had creamy pineapple flavours and a restrained use of oak, while a dry Ruländer Spätlese 1990 had a pleasant, spicy bouquet.

Nittnaus' reds start with his strawberry and toffee-flavoured St-Laurent. His Blaufränkisch wines are tannic and long, which is quite an achievement with this grape which is often neither. The Ried Haideboden 1990 had a little aftertaste of caraway seeds, while the wine from Ungerberg was full of dark blackcurrant and raspberry fruit and thick enough to be cut with a knife. It will need years. A *cuvée* of Cabernet, Blaufränkisch and St-Laurent is made too; but Nittnaus' pride and joy is his huge, tannic Cabernet of which 1989 was the first vintage. The 1990 should not be broached until sometime at the beginning of the next century; sadly, it will have been consumed by then. He makes a few sweet wines too, including a proper *Ausbruch* from Welschriesling, Sauvignon Blanc and Ruländer. The 1989 tasted of apricots and peaches. An *Eiswein* is occasionally made; the 1990 had a lovely taste of crystallized fruits.

Josef Umathum of Frauenkirchen is another name that can lead to genuflection in certain wine-appreciating circles in Vienna. He makes a couple of good whites from Ruländer and a blend of Ruländer and Weissburgunder which he calls the Pinot Cuvée. The straight Ruländer is good and spicy, with the weight to make it a fitting accompaniment to foie gras.

The Pinot Cuvée is nicely structured and full of flavour. Umathum's lightest red is his Zweigelt with its pepper, lentilly raspberry and cassis fruit. The rest of his reds seem to be hewn from blocks of stone. The only other varietal released separately is the St-Laurent which, with its brown sugar, violet and strawberry aromas, is almost certainly one of the best available. His top red is the *cuvée* which is made from Cabernet Sauvignon, Zweigelt and Blaufränkisch. All three are matured separately in cask and then blended. I have tried only the assemblages for the 1990 and 1989 vintages; wines so big that they are certain to last for years.

Geography masters face the unenviable new task of telling their charges that the capital city of the new state of Slovenia is called Ljubljana, and I can quite appreciate the Austro-German insistence on using the old name of Laibach: it is a good deal easier to pronounce. Illmitz, in the southern Seewinkel, has a special relationship with Ljubljana-Laibach: whenever one of the villagers visits the Slovenian capital he seems to come back with a gold medal. The only explanation for this largesse on the part of the Slovenians is that they must have very sweet teeth, for it is a peculiarity of the climate here that anything left unattended for two minutes turns to liquid sugar.

The Illmitz produce that Slovenians most like is of course wine, and chiefly *Beerenauslesen* and *Trockenbeerenauslesen*. Many of these wines are made by part-time winemakers like **Alois Kracher** of the Weinlaubenhof, who also pounds pills in a pharmaceutical firm in Vienna. Kracher is not modest about his wines: "Do you think they are better than Château d'Yquem?", he asked me. It is hard to know how to answer that sort of question. "Ah, different," I said, trying to be diplomatic; "I don't think Count Alexandre de Lur-Saluces has much Scheurebe."

Cuttings from local papers cover Kracher's cellar walls. In the Seewinkel they do not have my Anglo-Saxon reticence: they say he is very definitely better than Yquem.

Kracher's wines are all individual, like the man himself. All of them, dry whites and reds alike, have *Botrytis* tastes and some of the reds are disturbingly sweet. Then there are the grapes: Muskat-Ottonel, Bouvier and Scheurebe, which I simply dislike in nine-tenths of their incarnations. There were quite a few wines I liked among the 27 I tasted that afternoon, such as the Scheurebe Beerenauslese 1988 with its attractive cooked-pear character; the 1986 Scheurebe Beerenauslese with its lychee fruit and another Scheurebe Beerenauslese, which Kracher had put into Acacia wood. It seemed to me that Scheurebe was tolerable in these forms or when it gives grapefruit aromas, rather than the usual stench of incontinent pussy cats.

Kracher can vinify Muskat-Ottonel well too, and his party-trick is to bring out a small *Bocksbeutel* with 350 grams of residual sugar which he has to

Left: Reed stacks on the shores of the Neusiedlersee in Illmitz. Willi Opitz uses the reeds to make his Schilfmandl *wine. Below: A typical Burgenland maize-drier in Gols.*

pummel out of the bottle like tomato ketchup. In 1989 he made a nice Bouvier Beerenauslese which for once had acidity and length. A 1981 Gewürztraminer Beerenauslese had more class with its beeswax and apricot fruit. On the whole, however, I feel that Welschriesling gives him the best results, as in the Trockenbeerenauslese 1988 with its aroma of broom flowers.

Willi Opitz is Kracher's cousin. Opitz works in a pet-food factory during the day and spends his holidays in a vineyard the size of three football pitches. His wines are made by a careful grading of all the berries on a bunch: the healthy ones make dry whites and *Spätlese*, the *Botrytis*-affected ones make *Auslese, Beerenauslese* and *Trockenbeerenauslese* and those that do not rot are turned into 'reed wine' (dried on reeds), or left on the vines to make *Eiswein*.

The reed wine (*Schilfwein* in German) is Opitz's own invention and, even if he had done nothing else, he would be notable for this. A 1989 Welschriesling Schilfwein with 107 grams of residual sugar was superbly tangy, rather like good *Eiswein*. Once again, Welschriesling gives good results for this sort of wine. A Welschriesling Eiswein 1990 had lovely, tangy spiced-plum aromas, while a 1978 tasted of ripe mangoes.

Opitz is always inventing something. In 1982 he made a *Dreikönigswein* on 6 January. He is rare in using Grüner Veltliner for higher *Prädikat* wines, but the results are good, as was proved by a Beerenauslese 1988 which tasted of toffee and raisins. Even Muskat-Ottonel can be enobled in this way, as in the 1975, with its aromas of mandarin oranges, or a Beerenauslese 1981 which smelled of brown bread with caraway seeds. A Bouvier Trockenbeerenauslese 1981 put me in mind of figgy duff.

One of his most peculiar wines is a Weissburgunder he has had in cask for 12 years which tastes like a classic old *rancio*. Occasionally Opitz even uses red wines to make an *Eiswein* or a *Schilfwein*. The Blauburger Eiswein 1990 was a real stunner with its tangy plum-skin character. The Schilfmandl 1989 was also delicious with its 200 grams of residual sugar and its tastes of warm plums and raisins. They are an eccentric lot, these Illmitzers, but not without qualities.

CENTRAL BURGENLAND
(MITTELBURGENLAND)

Central Burgenland sticks out like a great pot belly into the western border of Hungary. As an area it is largely plain, relieved occasionally by a range of sleek hills. Viticulturally, the Blaufränkisch is king here, although in the past decade many growers have recognised that the grape can be a little short and age too quickly. This has led some to experimentation with other varieties; most notably the Cabernet Sauvignon. The main centres for quality production are to the east; in the villages of Neckenmarkt, Horitschon and Deutschkreuz.

Tibor Szemes runs his business from Pinkafeld in South Burgenland, but he buys his grapes in Horitschon and vinifies them at the cooperative before bringing them to Pinkafeld to mature in cask or tank. Szemes is a *négociant-éléveur*, a rare concept for modern Austria. All his growers have

Ried Hochäcker, the best vineyard in Horitschon.

contracts and he controls the pruning of the vines and gives premiums for the best grapes. He sets a lot of store by his nicely pear and raspberry flavoured *Schankwein* (the house wine which he sells to a number of outlets, including the Austrian equivalent of the British Happy Eater).

All Szemes' wine is Blaufränkisch and he even sells a little to Schlumberger Sekt to make their rosé. Szemes makes two qualities, one aged in large oak and the other in small *barriques*. The 1990 vintage was probably his best to date; many of the wines in cask had a charming blackcurrant pastille and raspberry fruit. The Reserve wines are housed in Nevers oak which gives them rather creamy flavours. Szemes' best old vintage was the 1986 (the 1983 is already showing signs of fading), of which there is a pleasantly round *barrique* wine. Both the 1987 and 1988 vintages suffered a little from the weather which showed up some of those Blaufränkisch short-comings.

Burgenland used to be called German West Hungary, and Szemes' name points out his racial

Spring scene in the vineyards of Central Burgenland. Central Burgenland's wines are 95 percent red; the Blaufränkisch vine predominating. Recently, however, growers have begun to experiment with French vines; chiefly the Cabernet Sauvignon.

origins. The 'Hungarian', Franz Liszt, was born in Raiding to a Hungarian-speaking father and German-speaking mother. Hungarians here tend to worship the old Habsburg monarchy and Szemes himself places effigies of Habsburg princes in all the key positions in his house and cellars.

One suspects that the Second World War and the minute size of the old village houses put paid to the old architecture in the villages; there is little left now. Horitschon is not an attractive place: permanently grey and dirty and dominated by an ugly modern church. **Franz Weninger** is the most talked about winemaker in the place, although his winemaking can be a touch hit or miss. Weninger aims specifically at cask flavours, indeed he prides himself on being the first Austrian to import Kentucky oak (the flavour is not far from many Austrian white oaks: a case of the emperor's new clothes). Zweigelt gets its banana flavours from wood; a Blaufränkisch with a nice, freshly milled black-pepper bouquet was being submerged with vanilla oak aromas. I found that I was more interested in the wines which were standing up for themselves: Tinavera was the top Blaufränkisch *cuvée* and had some nice violet aromas. There have also been two or three Cabernet Sauvignon vintages and the results look good.

Toni Iby is a part-time winemaker, but he has a full-time wife who looks after the commercial side and a Hungarian who tramps across the border every morning to see to the vines and cellar during his absence. His is a red-wine house and most of his wine is Blaufränkisch. The Zweigelt is good here, however, and Iby has harvested three vintages of a promising Blauburgunder. Iby says his wines undergo a complete malolactic fermentation, but I find the acidity levels on his reds still astonishingly high. In good years he makes a Jahrgangsreserve, of which the 1989 was a good wine. Some wine inevitably goes into small, new oak; again the 1989 is noteworthy. Older vintages show how Blaufränkisch changes its character with age: the 1986 and 1983 vintages all had a damp-leaf and rose-petal bouquet associated with very mature wine.

The **Weinkellerei**, or cooperative, in Horitschon is part of a movement to improve the image of the Mittelburgenland by cutting yields to around 50 hl/ha. Another of its ideas is to select annually the top 20 Blaufränkisch wines from the best villages. The cooperative itself makes reliable unoaked wines. The best of the rest seem to be from **Paul Kerschbaum** (Salon winner for 1991), with his leathery 1989, and **Paul Lehrner**, who made a quite delicious 1989 from the Ried Hochäcker. The Winzergenossenschaft in Neckenmarkt was also responsible for some decent wines.

There are lots of Wieders in Neckenmarkt, about 30 families all in all, including **Juliane Wieder**. Her Blaufränkisch was singled out by *Falstaff* magazine in 1990 – though I found it rather light – (did not Shakespeare's Falstaff give the advice to "forswear thin potations"?). **Stefan Wieder** is thought to be one of the best winemakers in the village. Quite a lot of Wieder's Blaufränkisch wines do not go through a malolactic fermentation, as he feels this can spoil the traditional character of the grape. When the acidity is overpowering, however, he does do a malolactic. Wieder's young wines have nice, classic white-pepper-and-raspberry aromas, including his Ried Sinter which was chosen for the Salon. Some of the wines go into small oak. Wieder makes a good Blaufränkisch brandy which he ages for two years in cask.

Engelbert Gesellmann has a problem: he thinks I am Anthony Rose of the *The Independent* newspaper, but there his problems end. This year he was one of *Falstaff* magazine's best Austrian winemakers and a lot of good things come out of his rather haphazard cellars in Deutschkreuz, a permanently gloomy, dusty town on the Hungarian border. Gesellmann makes a few successful white wines such as a nuts and honey-scented Weissburgunder 1990, or his Chardonnay, of which he makes convincing oaked and unoaked versions. In Indian summers, Gesellmann makes a *Beerenauslese* or *Trockenbeerenauslese* from Welschriesling. The 1970 was quite lovely, as was a Scheurebe Eiswein 1989 with a very acceptable grapefruit flavour.

Obviously the reds are the most important thing. In 1990 he made a fabulously rich, strawberry-scented Zweigelt and he sets considerable store by his Blauburgunder. 1990 was a very good year for Gesellmann's Blaufränkisch wines from the simplest to the top wine of the Ried Hochäcker with its heavy loam soils. The 1989 Hochäcker was also very fine with a slight taste of figs. Some of the wine is housed in small oak and this seems to pay off in vintages like 1986 when the flavours were rounded off by the cask. Like many Austrian winemakers, Gesellmann throws together three grape varieties in a *cuvée*. In this case Blaufränkisch, St-Laurent and Cabernet Sauvignon go into his Opus Eximium. Gesellmann also makes a Cabernet, but

again I was able to taste only two babies, which were both closed up.

Hans Igler's cellars are also in unlovely Deutschkreuz. Igler is a very careful winemaker who makes extremely tightly constructed wines which must age very slowly; sadly I see them every day on restaurant wine lists in Austria and they are simply not ready to drink. If I were an Austrian restaurateur, I would put some of the simpler wines on my list and forget about the others in my cellar. The simpler wines would be the strawberry-scented St-Laurent, of which the 1989 is ready, and the non-oaked Blaufränkisch, such as the 1989 and 1988 vintages. The 1986 straight Blaufränkisch is the best in this series, with its nice hints of violets, raspberries and cassis. "Hint" is the word here: nothing is overstated *bei* Igler.

The elect range begins with the Cuvée Vulcano in which 75 percent Blaufränkisch and 25 percent Cabernet Sauvignon is aged in cask. The wines are grown on gravelly soil and the "volcano" refers only to the 'breakthrough' represented by such a wine and not to anything geological. The 1988 here has a nice cassis note, but it needs lots of time. The same is true of a *barrique*-aged 1986 Blaufränkisch. Igler started making a straight Cabernet in 1987.

Deutschkreuz on the Hungarian border, the last of Central Burgenland's wine villages.

SOUTH BURGENLAND
(SÜDBURGENLAND)

South Burgenland is an agreeable, remote place which reminds me of certain parts of Ireland. The people are light-hearted, friendly and often eccentric. As far as wine is concerned, there seems to be a general readiness to help one another. As a result, winemakers are always sharing one another's wisdom and equipment. There is not much great wine here, but there is quite a lot of good wine in Deutsch Schützen or on the Eisenberg (a hill which looks out over the whole western Hungarian plain). Good whites come from Rechnitz and in the south there is the illegal wine, *Uhudler*, which is made from a lot of weird and wonderful grape varieties descended from vines imported from the United States in the last century.

The **Wallner** family of Deutsch Schützen make an awful lot of different wines for a 1.5-hectare estate. They use Welschriesling and Müller-Thurgau for whites and Zweigelt and Blaufränkisch for reds. The Zweigelt is a reliable cherry-scented wine, but their best is certainly the Blaufränkisch. 1990 is their best year to date and the wines have classic fruit. Some of the 1990s have been put into oak, as was the 1986, which had the effect of rounding it off nicely. The 1983 Falstaff wine is still on good form.

The Arkadenhof domaine is typical of South Burgenland. It mixes pig-farming with arable land and there is a *Buschenschank* plus 3.5 hectares of vines tended by young **Franz Wachter**. Wachter, like the Wallners, has a nice line in Zweigelts. Again 1990 was a propitious year for Blaufränkisch and Wachter experimented with different styles, bottling some early and adding press wine to another barrel. The 1989 Kabinett was a success, with a hint of blackcurrant. In 1990 Wachter made a Goldburger Strohwein (ie a *vin de paille*, or *recioto*-style wine). The grapes were laid out on straw for

The Eisenberg in South Burgenland. The hill looks out over the Hungarian Puszta.

five and a half months and then pressed, giving a dense bouquet of apricots and honey.

Giesela Wiesler's estate in Deutsch Schützen was one of the very first to attract attention to the remote Südburgenland. Sadly, in recent years the wines have often missed out on effective treatment in the cellar so that a strong reductive character develops in the tuns. The levels of carbon dioxide are also high, even in old wines, which leads one to suspect that they are not racked. Still, there is a nice Welschriesling/Müller-Thurgau blend which is fat and aromatic, and the straight Welschrieslings are less angular than most. The old wines seem to have preserved well, with an interesting cassis character emerging in the 1980 Blaufränkisch. The 1981 is the best wine here; it was kept on its *marc* for three months, producing a big nose of sweet blackcurrants. After that I would recommend the 1984 and 1985 vintages for their typicity. The best recent vintage was the 1987 Kabinett. Frau Wiesler has recently asked her young cousin Franz Wachter to help out in the cellar, and this should ensure that a little more care and attention is lavished on the wines in cask.

One small, mixed-culture domaine which has come to the fore in the past few months is that of the **Kopfensteiner** family. I tasted three of their 1990s over some good goats' cheese made on the nearby Eisenberg. Good cheese is a rare thing in Austria and rarest of all in Burgenland, so the goats' cheese came as a pleasant surprise. The wine too was impressive: the lightest Blaufränkisch Qualitätswein had interesting coffee/cherry notes, while a stronger wine had more powerful white-pepper and cherry aromas. A third *cuvée* had been put into oak with the hulls of some Blaufränkisch vinified as a rosé; this was the most promising of the lot.

Down the hill the **Körper** family and their son-in-law, Walter Faulhammer, run a guest house and seven-hectare estate. A great many investments have been made recently and the winemaking is of a high quality. Walter Faulhammer is a quiet man but clearly, still waters run deep, as I discovered on a late tour of some of Deutsch Schützen's nightspots. The Körpers are rare in the region for having old Rhine Riesling vines which make quite elegant lime-scented wines in good years, such as 1990. The red wines are now made in rotating vats, which

means that they have quite powerful tannins, rendering the younger wines hard to assess. I predicted a good future for a 1990 Blaufränkisch Kabinett with some cassis on the nose. Another oddity here is a pure Merlot wine, made from 25-year-old vines which give classic fruitcake-like aromas. The Körpers are also proud of their old wines such as a 1983 Blauburger Kabinett with dark chocolate aromas and a remarkably fresh 1979 Zweigelt.

Possibly the best of all the Deutsch Schützen estates is that owned by the family of the local politician and farmer **Hermann Krutzler**. As in so many local cases, the agriculture here is mixed, with a good deal of arable land and, from what it sounds like, when they sing for their supper in the early hours of the afternoon, a remarkable number of pigs. Hermann Krutzler is seconded by his sons: Erich works on the domaine while another of the three is learning winemaking in Eisenstadt.

Blaufränkisch is once again the top wine here. Like the Kopfensteiners, the Krutzlers make a rosé and feed back the hulls into a red wine. This method was used with the 1990 Ried Weinberg, giving it good, complex fruit. Another 1990 from the Eisenberg was a powerful brew with a bouquet of morello cherries. The top Blaufränkisch is blended with some ten percent Cabernet Sauvignon to lengthen the palate and provide better ageing potential. This appears to be a wise policy all

in all. The first such experiment was carried out in 1988; in 1989 the same blend was easily their best wine; and in 1990 the blend was well-structured and promising.

The Krutzlers use a palette of different oaks including some from Burgenland. Burgenland oak is a white oak, and this was very obvious in the top 1987 wine which was made without Cabernet. The best Krutzler old wines are the 1983s: a Kabinett with a brown-sugar bouquet and a Spätlese with raspberry and strawberry tastes as yet undiminished by time.

Before we leave Südburgenland, a passing reference should be made to the wines of the deep south which are made in the villages of Heiligenbrunn and Moschendorf. Although there *are* 'normal' wines made in these southern communes near the old fortified town of Güssing, the fame of the vineyards rests on the production of *Uhudler* (*see p* 28) which is produced from American vines, chiefly Noah, Ripatella, Otello, Elvira (shades of *Blythe Spirit*), Hinkton (known here as the *Italiener*), Hönigler (which seems to have lost its American name along the way), Seibel and Concord.

Since the time of Kurt von Schuschnigg, and indeed Adolf Hitler, there have been serious attempts to stamp out *Uhudler*. Finally, in 1965, a law was passed forbidding its sale. The legislators arm themselves with the 'fact' that *Uhudler* is actually harmful to the health if drunk in any quantity. This is apparently untrue, and *Uhudler* contains no more methanol than any other red or white wine. Recently *Uhudler* producers have been coming out of the woodwork more and more and the *Uhudler* tasting I attended in Moschendorf was an example of a new temerity.

The first major difference between *Uhudler* and any other wine lies in the texture of the grapes themselves. The skins and the pulp easily detach themselves from one another leaving the famous 'foxy' flavour of the American grapes. This should not be assumed to be anything like the smell of the animal: anything which smelled that bad would be undrinkable. The aromas I associate with *Uhudler* grapes correspond more to synthetic strawberry and cherry flavourings such as one might find in bubble-gum. It is not at all disagreeable, as I discovered in the best Noah whites and Ripatella reds.

Uhudler wines are remarkably difficult to obtain unless you have an introduction to one of the producers. If indeed it is harmless (these vines are freely cultivated in the United States), I can see no reason why these immensely jolly people in Moschendorf and Heiligenbrunn should not continue making the stuff until doomsday; or indeed drinking themselves under the table on it every Saturday night.

STYRIA
(STEIERMARK)

WESTSTEIERMARK

SÜD-OSTSTEIERMARK

Graz

Riegersburg

Fehring

Ligist

Kapfenstein

Greisdorf   St-Stefan

Stainz

Straden

Deutschlandsberg   St-Andrä   SÜD-

Klöch

Leibnitz

STEIERMARK   Ehrenhausen

Bad Radkersburg

Ratsch

Eibiswald

Schlossberg

Major vine-growing areas

Wine routes

SOUTHEAST STYRIA
(SÜD-OSTSTEIERMARK)

Burgenland attaches itself to Styria at the foot and without one perceiving the change in landscape; suddenly a sign announces the onset of Styria – the land of pumpkins, pumpkin oil and quaintly dressed backwoodsmen. The wine *appellation* Southeast Styria is large and rambling and only a few patches of quality vines justify its inclusion. These are gathered in the Grosslage Vulkanland, which juts out like a spur into the old Yugoslav provinces of Slovenia and Croatia. The best of these vines line the hills running along the borders.

After 1985 Styria was greeted as the promised land by all those people who had felt betrayed by the behaviour of the fraudsters. The Styrian wine-makers had been in no way implicated; their climate did not easily allow them to make the sort of *lieblich* wines so easy to fabricate with chemicals.

The autumn pumpkin-seed harvest in Styria.

Suddenly Styrian wine was the most sought-after of all Austria's wines and this is how it has remained.

Styria had not enjoyed fame of this sort since before 1918 when the wines had been drunk throughout the Habsburg Empire. The territorial settlement of Versailles allocated the major part of the old province to Yugoslavia and that included most of the best estates. As a result, few of the current new-wave producers have either history or old wines, but there are exceptions and some of these are to be found in Süd-Oststeiermark.

The most notable old domaine in the area is the **Gräflich Stürgkh'sches Weingut** in Klöch. Countess Ladislaja Stürgkh married former ambassador Baron Georg Seyffertitz and it is his son Cari Seyffertitz who now looks after the wine-making. Stürgkh is a ruined castle which towers over the old village of Klöch; the Seyffertitz's modern house is above the old cellars below the ruins. It is quite a climb up to the house, as I discovered on a freezing February day when my car

Top: The cellars at Schloss Stürgkh, justly famous for Gewürztraminer.
Above: Manfred Platzer's fibreglass fermenters.

had shown a remarkably tenacious affection for a ditch on the side of the road. Stürgkh is a white-wine house. Many of the estate wines were showing heavy levels of sulphur dioxide that day, but I was impressed by a classy Rhine Riesling and a very good Sauvignon Blanc with a smoky, artichoke character. The speciality here has long been the Gewürztraminer, which develops a bouquet of yellow roses and gingerbread. A 1966 was still very fresh with lots of honey, wild herbs and ginger-bread on the bouquet. Seyffertitz also makes schnapps. A quince schnapps proved remarkably useful prior to facing the Arctic temperatures out-side the house that February day.

Manfred Platzer is not far away in Tieschen. He is a careful, technically proficient winemaker with a passion for mechanical wizardry. Platzer makes some very clean white wines, such as his aniseed-scented Welschriesling 1990 and a remar-

kably good Weissburgunder Sekt called Vision (several Styrian winemakers have banded together and enjoy the right to make this wine) which has a pleasant touch of paprika on the bouquet. Some of the *Sekt* is enhanced with elderflowers, giving it a rather herby character. Weissburgunder is, in general, good here, some of the wine going into barrels of Allier or Styrian oak. The latter comes from Platzer's own woods; so I suppose we may call it *Platzereiche*.

Other whites of note are a Rhine Riesling and a classic Styrian Gelber Muskateller with a lemony character. Like Stürgkh, Platzer makes very good Gewürztraminer with some *Spätlesen* and *Auslesen* producing caraway aromas added to the more usual radish-and-yellow-rose bouquet. The best of the lot was a 1989 Auslese. In general, the 1989 vintage was better here than in many other parts of Austria.

Platzer is rare in this part of the country for making creditable reds. Even a simple Zweigelt 1990 had lashings of flavour, while three St-Lau-rents proved that he understood this grape well enough to bring out its strawberry-coffee aromas.

*Riegersburg in Southeast
Styria. The village is not
known for its wines; but in
Johann Zieser, it boasts one of
the country's best schnapps
distillers.*

Pretty castles are not rare in Styria. The hills seem to have been designed for some crown of stone; the residence of a feudal magnate in what still feels like feudal country. **Georg Winkler-Hermaden**, however, does not strike me as much of a feudalist; I cannot quite see him insisting on his rights to *jus primae noctis* in Kapfenstein. The castle itself has been turned into an hotel, run by Georg's brother; there are good reports on the quality of the food.

Most of the Winkler-Hermaden wines are white, with a classy Rhine Riesling and a good, fruity Weissburgunder. A Ruländer is housed in Kapfenstein oak (!) and has a nice, spicy bouquet. Winkler-Hermaden occasionally makes impressive Sauvignon Blancs and I was much taken with his asparagus-scented 1988. The Gewürztraminers can also be good. A rosé serves as a hyphen between the whites and the reds here, and it is one of the best I have tasted in Austria. It is made from Zweigelt, like his red wines; Winkler-Hermaden gets good colour and fruit flavour from this grape. He also makes some impressive grappa-style schnapps.

The industrious **Johann Zieser** of Riegersburg specialises in schnapps. He plucks his cherries, apples, quinces or raspberries undamaged from the trees or canes. Consequently, his *Kirsch* (cherry), *Glockenapfel* (a local apple variety), *Quitte* (quince) and *Himbeer* (raspberry) fetch prodigious prices at Austria's top hotels and restaurants.

It is always a pleasure to taste wines with a meal. A meal is, after all, the perfect setting for good wine. But tasting wines with food has one considerable drawback: it is neither desirable nor decorous to spit wine out and if you do not spit, the afternoon becomes long and arduous. Still, I have very fond memories of a wine-tasting meal at Straden, a pretty village with a great many onion-domed churches, in Southeast Styria. My hosts were **Albert and Anni Neumeister**, who have about six hectares of vines and a *Buschenschank*.

The meal was not, however, the usual porky *Buschenschank* food. The Neumeisters had enlisted the help of a local chef of some talent to prepare the meal. A rabbit's liver with sweetbreads and a lambs lettuce salad was the first dish to appear, the wine

99

was a slightly vegetal Welschriesling from the volcanic soils of the Ried Saziani. With a frothy Riesling soup came a cask sample of Rhine Riesling with a good lime bouquet. Then a Sauvignon Blanc 1989 fermented in new oak accompanied some chicken breasts wrapped in cabbage with dill sauce. The Sauvignon Blanc, with its artichoke character, has won some fame for the Neumeisters.

A 1989 Zweigelt was matched with a piece of pork fillet with horn-of-plenty mushrooms and potato cakes. The wine was very good, with flavours of cloves and blackberries. Later they brought out the 1990 which was even better. Our dessert was a *Kaiserschmarren* (*see p* 28) which came with a glass of spicy Ruländer Kabinett 1987 and later some Gewürztraminer from the same vintage. Now, I cannot remember for the life of me what I did for the rest of that afternoon.

WEST STYRIA
(*WESTSTEIERMARK*)

Ask a Viennese what goes on in West Styria and he will say: "Oh, that's *Schilcher* country."

"*Schilcher*?", you reply in all innocence; "What's *Schilcher*?"

"What! You've never tasted *Schilcher*? My! You've got a treat in store!"

But somehow you are not wholly convinced that they are not just pulling your leg.

Schilcher is indeed a speciality of West Styria; it is made almost nowhere else and rarely do bottles of it even migrate to other parts of the Republic. *Schilcher* is not only a West Styrian wine, it is practically a West Styrian acquired taste. The other great speciality is pumpkin-seed oil. Travel through the hilly West Styrian countryside in autumn and you will see vineyards, full of ripe (well almost ripe) grapes, snaking down the steep hillsides and between them little old ladies in headscarves sitting on mounds of green and orange pumpkins viciously hewing them in half with machete-like knives and scooping out the seeds. The rest of the pumpkin is apparently inedible and is then discarded in the field; left for the Siberian crows.

Schilcher was explained to me in the Jagawirt restaurant in Greisdorf. Here a young producer,

who also works for the Landwirtschaftskammer (Chamber of Agriculture), told me all about the Blauer Wildbacher grape which makes the sharp rosé wines of *Schilcher*. Over my chanterelle soup with polenta dumplings he told me about the 260 hectares of Wildbacher and the nature of this grape famed for its acidity of 10 or 11 g/l. Some of the wine from the best producers comes with a protective seal depicting a white horse: one of the famous Lipizzaner horses of the Spanish Riding School in Vienna; the horses are bred in West Styria.

Above: The harvest in Styria. Since the scandal of 1985 Styria has become the most fashionable wine-producing region in Austria; famous for its sappy, dry white wines.

Left: The monastery at Stainz in West Styria. West Styria's speciality is a sharp rosé wine called Schilcher *made from the Blauer Wildbacher grape.*

The best Schilcher *can make a good, refreshing drink which goes well with rich food.*

Then came my venison cutlet with red cabbage, *Spätzle* noodles and cep sauce and my first glass of *Schilcher* from **Max Grinschgl**. The wine had a nice smell of strawberries and a taste of green tomatoes with the acidity of a sprig of wild sorrel: "The first glass should not taste of anything", said my host in a consolatory way.

The Wildbacher grape has a long history. Records trace it back for more than 500 years in this region and, apart from a 20-hectare vineyard somewhere in the Veneto in Italy, it exists nowhere else.

The man began to get lyrical as my *Schilchertorte* arrived: the Wildbacher was a relative of the Cabernet Sauvignon, he said, and should taste a little like the Bordeaux grape. I did not answer this provocative contention and bit into my tart. Later I asked for the recipe, but the *Wirt* said it was a secret and that was that.

We decided that the best way to get to grips with *Schilcher* was to visit a producer. The **Lazarus** family lives above a very modern *Buschenschank* in St-Stefan ob Stainz. They have 8.5 hectares of vines, of which 90 percent is Wildbacher. We tasted a *Schilcher* which was still in cask. It was a deep rose colour and tasted herby. The rest of the 1990s bottles tasted revealed flavours of grass, rhubarb and gooseberries. So far I had not found the flavour of blackcurrants which organoleptically linked it with Cabernet, but I did not dislike it for all that. We even tried a *Schilcher* brandy which had a slightly grassy nose.

We went to Bad Gams, next to Wildbach itself, where Schubert composed the mawkish song about the trout. Here was a grower called **Johann Koller** who farmed some of the vineyards below the *Schloss* (wines to drink with trout perhaps?). Here indeed was a little taste of cassis mingled with the grass and rhubarb. We even tried an old *Schilcher*, as our guide was convinced that a friend of mine had been quite passionate about bottle-aged

Ried Burgegg in Deutschlandsberg. Vineyards once owned by the Liechtenstein family now belong to Günter Müller.

Schilcher (she denied this later): the 1982 was rather orangey and quite sharp with a slight bottle-stink. I thought I would stick to the young version: *Schilcher* should be fresh.

The biggest man in West Styria is **Günter Müller** in Gross St-Florian. Müller lives in a large house with several children and a collection of animals including a large, flop-eared hare. A part of Müller's business is importing wines from all over the world and he is responsible for supplying the Austrians with Bollinger champagne, Domaine de La Romanée Conti burgundies and Delamain cognacs. As far as his vineyards are concerned, only a part are in West Styria and those are the former possessions of the Liechtenstein family who used to own the mediaeval fortress above Deutschlandsberg. Müller had been renting them for some time before death duties in Austria forced the reigning princes to sell out. Some Liechtensteins still live in the more comfortable-looking *Schloss* at the bottom of the hill. The rest of Müller's vines are in

South Styria and he has a little red wine in Burgenland.

As a merchant as well as a grower Müller has three qualities of *Schilcher*: the first comes from the best grapes from his Liechtenstein vineyards (the second best from here go to make his very successful Schilcher Sekt); the second is wine from bought-in grapes and is sold to supermarkets, and the third quality is wine bought in cask which is traded somewhere behind the scenes, Müller was not anxious to say where. The Liechtenstein Schilcher had a taste of unripe blackcurrants: maybe it is Cabernet Sauvignon!

Müller makes other wines on his Liechtenstein slopes, including a dry Ruländer with a floral, tobacco nose (Virginia) and a marmelady Gewürztraminer. The Gewürztraminer was planted in 1948; that same year Dr Zweigelt planted some of his own Zweigelt vines on the slopes of Burgegg below the fortress walls. Zweigelt had been dismissed by the Allied authorities from his director-ship of the Klosterneuburg school because of his collaboration with the Nazis after the Anschluss. The Liechtensteins must have generously employed his talents on their estate.

It was interesting to try these original Zweigelt wines. The 1989 had a chocolate and cherry aroma with a slight touch of pepper; it was clearly a classic. Yields, it goes without saying, are extremely low.

Müller makes a nice Welschriesling with a good steely structure from his vineyard in Gamlitz on the Slovenian border. His current infatuation is his vineyard at Ottenberg in South Styria, from which came a catty Sauvignon Blanc and an impressive oak-aged, modern-style Chardonnay. Naturally, he has a Cabernet Sauvignon too (with 12 percent Merlot) grown on graphite. The 1989 was a bit too closed to assess when I tried it in 1991.

Schloss Liechtenstein, Hollenegg. The Liechtensteins, rulers of the principality between Austria and Switzerland, sold out recently because of crippling death duties.

SOUTH STYRIA
(SÜDSTEIERMARK)

South Styria is the smallest of the Styrian *appellations*. Conversely, it contains the largest number of vineyards (1,560 hectares) and the best producers. Hard by the Slovenian border is a group of growers whose names are recited in a sort of litany in wine circles in the capital. Asked to describe the virtues of these boutique wines, restaurateurs and writers refer generally to their 'juiciness', but clearly another virtue is the angular structure and high acidity of the best Styrian wines. There are very few sweet wines made here. Their popularity has meant that prices have soared. Tell this to a man like Willi Sattler in Gamlitz and he roars with laughter: "Yes, and I'm thinking of putting up the prices again this vintage", he says. In the South Styrian *Weinstrasse* (wine route) it is, very simply, a seller's market.

Not all the wines are grown here on the border, with its rolling hills and vines which earn it the title of the 'Austrian Tuscany'; around Kitzeck there is a group of growers who can boast vineyards rising to 650 metres above sea-level. Here the **Kappel** family run a vineyard, hotel and restaurant. They make very fine Gelber Muskatellers, racy Rhine Rieslings (with slopes like these!) and a particularly good Morillon.

Morillon is the local name for the Chardonnay grape. Sometime in the last century a benefactor of the region (Archduke Johann's name has often been invoked) brought back some vines from Champagne. These vines were known by the name they had apparently possessed in France: Morillon. Some ten years ago ampelographers realised that these vines were in fact Chardonnay. The Styrians, though, continued to produce them as they always had; making well-structured, linear wines without the flavours derived from oak barrels.

In St-Andrä im Sausal **Franz Hirschmugl** farms a vineyard rented from the Baron Wucherer as well as his own 5 hectares of vines, making 9.5 hectares in all. Hirschmugl makes some nutty Weissburgunders and spicy Ruländers in vineyards which rise to over 600 metres. His Morillon is not one of the raciest, but he has a couple of Sauvignon Blancs which show some catty typicity.

Gamlitz, Styria; the source of some of Austria's most highly prized whites.

The 1990 *cuvée* has a grassy, asparagus palate.

The route to Gamlitz and the *Weinstrasse* proceeds through the village of Ehrenhausen, which is dominated by a splendid Renaissance *Schloss* and a church with a ravishing onion dome. The Sattlerhof is a few miles further on up a steep road in Sernau which can be a perilous drive in midwinter. The **Sattlers** have a wine estate and a restaurant which is considered one of the best in Styria (*see p* 121). It is a simple enough formula: a short menu and Sattler wines. A lemony Gelber Muskateller comes as an aperitif; an angular

From the South Styrian 'Weinstrasse' (wine route) near Spielfeld on the Slovenian border.

Welschriesling accompanies a beetroot soup with dill; while a peachy Weissburgunder comes with chicken on a bed of pumpkin with dumplings.

Sattler's most expensive wines are not served by the glass: they are in short supply even next door to the winery. I met the large, jolly winemaker, Sattler, one icy February; a time when there are few tourists in Styria and the restaurant is firmly closed. With the land he is now planting he will have nearly ten hectares of vines dotted around Sernau, Kranach and the Pfarrweingarten. Weiss-burgunder (called Klevner here) is one of his most important varieties. The 1986 had a pronounced chocolate flavour, other vintages are rather more truffly. Sattler makes some splendid Ruländers

which have a strong aroma of grapefruit, and a petrolly Rhine Riesling. His reds, made from 80 percent St-Laurent with 20 percent Zweigelt, are a surprise in this region, for they show a wide palette of fruits.

His pride and joy are the Morillons and Sauvignon Blancs. The Morillon is one of the best of its sort: the 1990 was clearly nicely structured but rather mute that freezing February day, only a few months after its birth. The 1989, with its jelly-baby nose, orangey fruit and great length, was easier to judge. The Sauvignon Blanc he calls "The King of Kings": the 1990 was certainly excellent with its asparagus bouquet and grassy palate.

I must confess I had a little problem with the wines of **Alois Gross** of Ratsch at first. When we arrived, in the middle of a blizzard, Gross was merrily melting a pig for lard in an outbuilding. The smell of this hot *Schmalz* was all-pervading, and it seemed to have got onto the dishcloth which had cleaned my glass. The first few wines had me thinking of hogs and little else; but the sharp Welschrieslings eventually had their effect and I eventually discovered some excellent wines.

Weissburgunder is a staple here too; the steep 400 metre-high slopes produce a spicy wine rather than the usual nutty one. A rarity is the Roter Riesling, with its orange and mushroom aromas. Sauvignon Blancs come from two *Riede*: Sulz and Nussberg. The first smelled of peaches and paprika, while in the second the paprika dominated. A 1989 was more fruit-salady and a 1984 had me thinking of green peas with mint. Some Ruländer is aged in wood to give it an orange cream character; a 1986 Spätlese was more reminiscent of pineapple with brown sugar. Gross has only a small amount of Morillon, but he is ripping out his promiscuous vineyard to plant more; the Kabinett 1989 was rather peachy with immense length.

Like many of his highly rated colleagues, **Manfred Tement** makes a wine with the intriguingly Prussian name of *Junker*. *Junker* is a blended or single-grape variety wine that is bottled early and marketed as a *primeur* like Beaujolais Nouveau. It is in very short supply and I fear it will be a while before it is discovered in Berlin. The name alludes, of course, to the origins of the word *Junker*, from *junger Herr* or young lord.

Tement is another of the top league producers on the *Weinstrasse*. His most widely planted grape is the Welschriesling with its rapier-like acidity. I find the Gelber Muskatellers to have more lemony charm. In terrain like this it comes as little surprise that the Rhine Riesling should prosper. Tement makes a good straight Weissburgunder with very appealing fruit and a Weissburgunder/Chardonnay blend (*he* calls it Chardonnay and not Morillon). A couple of Chardonnays from the 1990 vintage reveal his mastery of the grape. No oak is used and the wines have a rather bready intensity. The riper of the two (12.5°) had some good pineapple flavours.

Tement vinifies his Gewürztraminers in a rather light and unaromatic style (which I do not care for). Once again, the Sauvignon Blanc is considered to be one of Austria's best. The fruit grows on the steep slopes of Zieregg and Grassnitzberg which make longer-lasting, less aromatic wines than, say, Sancerre; moreover most of the vine-stock here was imported from Friuli. Tement made two 1990s: the cheaper of the two was slightly catty, the more expensive one had a faintly grassy bouquet and a tighter structure. A 1984 (a difficult vintage) had strong, asparagus character.

Reinhold Polz's 14-hectare domaine lies smack on the border with Slovenia. The amicable, if eccentric, lawyer who drove me there asked me if I have been to Slovenia. I said no. Suddenly he swung the car over to the other side of the road:

A Styrian grower using an old-fashioned and now rare basket press. Most growers are now investing in modern equipment.

"You're in Slovenia," he said. In the winemaking Rebenhof hotel, where I stayed that night, the manager was able to point to trees and winemakers' huts: "That's a border tree, and that hut there, that's in Slovenia," he said. The closeness to the border creates an odd, eery atmosphere, which contributes to the overall feeling of remoteness.

The Polz wines fetch high prices and they have very little to sell. When I arrived there were, apart from a red wine made from 50 percent Cabernet and 50 percent Blaufränkisch, only 1990s available. The wines were all in their first infancy, though I was able to see the tight structure of the Rhine Riesling and the spicy nature of the Weissburgunders. The Polz family make classic Styrian Morillons and show no interest in the international style. In 1990 they made two, both with great length and good, youthful Chardonnay character. The best of these comes from the Hochgrassnitzberg. The Sauvignon Blanc is marked by a strong cats'-pee character, which does not worry me at all in Sauvignon Blanc. Some Ruländer goes into new oak after fermentation in big tuns. The Polzs also make very good schnapps from their grapes and an apple schnapps from Golden Delicious apples.

I arrived to meet the **Lackner-Tinnachers** on the morning of Ash Wednesday. The night before I had said goodbye to meat at a real Styrian knees-up in Spielfeld. As cars and buildings disappeared beneath the snowflakes, the local school was host to a gathering of villagers in fancy dress: Tarzan,

Charlie Chaplin, Laurel and Hardy, several gorillas, a cowboy or two, Baron Ochs from *Der Rosenkavalier* and many more. This unlikely assembly danced into the small hours, stopping occasionally to bite the back out of a *Faschingskrapfen* before returning to the floor.

It was in a state of some shock that I arrived in Gamlitz at the rather smart property of the Lackner-Tinnachers. With 50 hectares of vines and fruit, they are rather big fish; I imagine they had prepared themselves for the 40 days of Lent in a more decorous way than I. They differ from neighbouring top properties in that they have neither Chardonnay nor Morillon wines, and, though they have some Sauvignon Blanc planted, it was vintaged first only in 1991.

The Lackner-Tinnachers make a lot of good wines. I was very taken with their Gelber Muskateller with its aromatic, lemony nose; this wine seemed to get better as it got older and a Spätlese 1983 was beautifully creamy. Spotless cleanliness marks wines like the Weissburgunder, which in the 1989 vintage had a 'church wax' character; the 1983 was benchmark wine with its violet aroma. There

are good Rhine Rieslings too: the 1989 should be excellent in a few years; the 1987 already is. The Gewürztraminers here are intense and not in the leaner style of many properties in South Styria.

Their best grape is undoubtedly the Ruländer. This they vinify in all styles from a light 1990 to a Spätlese from the same vintage with more spice. A Kabinett 1986 had a sweet apple character, while a 1989 Auslese was more honeyed. The Lackner-Tinnachers are rare here for producing wines with this *Prädikat* level; a 1986 Auslese was harvested on 1 December and was wonderfully honeyed. That same year they made an Eiswein with a classic taste of frost on its pineappley fruit. *Botrytis* comes about once a decade; in the 1980s it was the 1981 vintage and the Ruländer grape made a Beerenauslese tasting of honey, apricots, figs and peaches. Before that vintage it was the 1979, which once again had some of the aromas of a freshly polished church; or so it seemed – perhaps I was feeling holy after my carnival party in Spielfeld.

Ried Zieregg in South Styria. Günter Müller of Gross St-Florian is a major producer on these slopes.

CHAPTER III

The Foods of Austria

*M*uch of Austria has an antiquated feel about it, and Vienna itself seems all the more so; stuck in a time-warp with its old-fashioned courtesy and Old-World charm. Despite heavy war damage, Vienna emerged from the Hitler years with its familiar face intact; the few scars have now mostly healed, and, with a dab of cosmetic here and there, most people would never realise that so many of the city's baroque masterpieces were shattered by bombs. There is an air of permanence; returning to Vienna after decades away one is immediately at home in the smells and atmosphere of the capital. Along the Wien river runs the Naschmarkt, the river is covered now from the inner-city *Ring* to the Habsburg summer palace at Schönbrunn. Beside the *art nouveau* Sezession building the market stalls still exude the same acrid smells of brine-soaked gherkins and *Sauerkraut* mingled with the scents of those spices most closely associated with Viennese cuisine: cumin, caraway, dill, ginger, nutmeg, cinnamon, juniper and, above all, paprika.

The famous coffee houses have their own aromas; above all it is that welcome smell of freshly milled coffee which greets you as you pass through the heavily curtained door. A Viennese coffee house

A tub of sauerkraut *in Vienna's Naschmarkt.*

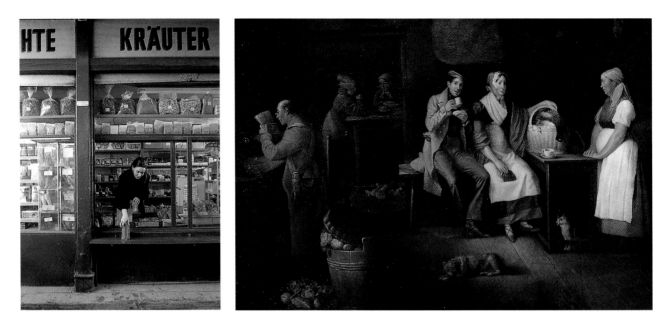

Left: A spice seller in the Naschmarkt.
Above: In der Kaffeeküche *by Nader, Wiener Historischers Museum; an image echoed in today's cafés.*

very rapidly becomes a home from home, or, as a recent Austrian book on the subject has called them, "an extended drawing room". Visit the same coffee house three times in a week and the *Kellner* begins to know your order; on the fourth occasion he will bring you a *Mokka* or a *Melange* before you have asked for it.

The ordinary Viennese eat at a *Gasthaus* or *Beisl*, an institution half-way between a pub and a café. These too have their distinctive smells; in the Gmoa Keller in the Heumarkt it is a pungent blend of decades of boiled cabbage mixed with a venerable strain of garlic. Not for nothing is garlic known here as "the poor man's vanilla" or "Hungarian vanilla", giving a clue to the origin of the three sisters who run the place. Spend an hour in a *Beisl* in the capital and the smells will settle on your clothes and remain there until you next get the chance to visit the dry cleaner.

You can eat virtually anywhere and at any time in Austria. In the wine regions *Buschenschenken* provide anyone wanting a drink with a range of snacks and meals. In the Viennese suburbs this role is performed by the *Heurigen*. A coffee house can generally rustle up a *Wiener Schnitzel*, some soup or an omelette. If you stop at the butcher to buy meat, there is often the chance to eat a brace of sausages before you leave. Cake shops provide a permanent source of temptation to the weak-willed in the major cities and for anyone who has over-

come these obstacles, there is always the *Würstelstand*. Sausage stalls can be found on just about every main junction in Austrian towns and cities. On the pavement by the Albertina Museum in Vienna, a stone's throw from both the Opera House and the famous Sacher Hotel, is the *Würstelstand* which the locals like to call the *Kleines Sacher* (little Sacher).

For anyone who has eaten a copious Viennese lunch the *Kleines Sacher* provides a cheap, wholesome dinner consisting of a hunk of *Leberkäse* or a couple of *Bratwurst*, a sliced *Grillwurst* (both of which are exceptional in that they are grilled or fried) or a fiery *Teufelswurst* (literally the devil's sausage). You will be given the choice of sweet or sour mustard (*süsser* or *scharfer Senf*) between bread or a roll (*Brot oder Semmel*).

Austria was the hub of the Habsburg Empire and Vienna was its imperial capital. Unlike the British Empire, the Austrian was not only wholly open to influences from its subject nations, it was dominated by them. The removal of the Turkish menace in 1683 meant a new relaxation when it came to trade. Vienna suddenly became a market for oysters, almonds, chestnuts, pistaccios, rice, currants, Spanish wines, Italian and Dutch cheeses,

Venetian confectionery, Indian spices, coffee and cocoa. Two centuries later the formal union of the Austrian and Hungarian crowns led to new waves of emigration to Vienna. On the one hand there were the Bohemians, who became the cobblers, tailors, cooks, nannies, lackies and NCOs of the empire; on the other were the Hungarians: aristocrats, officers, magnates, stud-farmers, musicians, artists, writers and *boulevardiers*. Both peoples brought with them elements important to Viennese cooking as we now know it: the Hungarians introduced *Gulyas* (gulasch), paprika and *Palatschinken* (pancakes); the Bohemian style was more homely: *Dalken* (thick pancakes baked in dripping), *Tascherl* (big pasta envelopes made from a potato flour dough), *Buchtel* (a yeast dough sponge), *Knödel* (dumplings) and *Powidl* (plum jam).

CAFÉ SOCIETY

Something of this split between the aristocratic Austrian-Magyar world and the plebeian Bohemian-provincial element is apparent in the contrast between the lethargic café world and the bustling atmosphere of the *Gasthaus*. Starting at breakfast time, whole days can be wasted in cafés; the *Kellner* is highly unlikely to ask you to move on, or vacate your place for another and one coffee allows you warmth (Viennese winters can be severe) and a liberal supply of newspapers. Some of the larger cafés in central Vienna even stock foreign papers such as *The Times*, *The Daily Mail*, *The Herald Tribune* and *Le Monde*.

The choice itself, however, is far from simple: there is no such thing as an ordinary 'coffee' and many of the larger cafés have lists of specialities. The basic black coffee is called a *Mokka*; a *Brauner* comes with milk, and a *Mélange* is roughly half milk, half coffee. Beyond the *Melange* are the most extravagent coffees: the Italian Cappuccino, sometimes given its German name of *Kapuziner*; the *Einspänner*, the most famous Viennese coffee, served in a tall glass with lashings of whipped cream; a *Pharisäer* comes with rum and whipped cream – and there are all sorts of others in which a tot of alcohol plays its role in giving you a mid-afternoon boost. Some cafés serve a particularly revolting coffee, supposedly favoured by one of the emperors, which involves beating a couple of egg yolks into the boiling beverage before serving.

Viennese residents have their own ideas about just what a *Kaffeehaus* should be, and styles vary considerably. Cafés range from the luxurious to the distinctly shabby. One of the best of the larger cafés (with the advantage of a large selection of newspapers) is the Landtmann, just opposite the Austrian Parliament building. With both the Burgtheater and the University nearby, the clientele tends to be a curious blend of politician, actor, artist and student. Like many of Vienna's old cafés, Landtmann has lately been redecorated and looks a little too austerely clean for all tastes. In the Josefstadt, behind the *Rathaus* (city hall), is the more

Below left: The Café Sperl in the Gumpendorfer Strasse.
Below: The Café Central, formerly the haunt of pre-1917 Russian revolutionaries.

authentically studenty Eiles with its blowsy blond waitress and large billiard room. Another fairly scruffy café is the Hawelka in the Dorotheergasse in the centre of the city. The Hawelka is nonetheless one of the most atmospheric of Vienna's *Kaffee-häuser*; its extraordinary parade of regulars continues from breakfast time to the early hours of the following morning.

BREAKFAST

For visitors to the city who are not happy with the breakfast provided by their hotels, the meal can be taken in a café such as the magnificent Sperl in the Gumpendorfer Strasse, or the Tirolerhof by the Albertina. The Viennese seem to think nothing of starting their day with a hunk of apple *Strudel*, and in the Tirolerhof it is often hard to fight off the urgent ministrations of the *Kellner* with his cakes. Breakfast tends to be sliced sausage and cheese everywhere this side of the Rhine, and Austria is no exception to the rule. Much of the sausage is highly garlicky, and the smell of that particularly Austrian seasoning early in the day is just something to which you will have to reconcile yourself.

Austrian bread can be an alternative to garlic sausage, or the curious *Käsewurst* (sausage with seams of cheese through it) which is popular in the Austrian countryside. There is an astonishing variety of bread available, even though much of it comes from the Anker bakers' shop chain. Anker is something of an institution in the capital and it is said that the Viennese abroad longs for "*Hochquell wasser und Ankerbrot*" (the pure city spring water and Anker bread). These days the unrestricted praise for Anker must be something of a rarity: the shop now has a virtual monopoly on bakers' shops, but in restaurants and in the country bread tends to be less mass-produced. In Burgenland, for example, the Barth-Stuben in Neusiedl am See presented baskets of sesame seed, walnut, wholemeal and white bread; other restaurants in the region offer the long, croissant-like *Stangl* covered with melted cheese or rock salt. In the wild south of the region *Stangl* is stuffed with *Grammeln* (the crunchy bits left over after the lard has been made) and baked in dripping. In Illmitz in the Seewinkel there used to be a long tradition of baking *Gebild-broten*, or large, decorated loaves, at festive times.

A stuffed bear cub in the Weisser Rauchfangkehrer restaurant in Vienna.

In Dürnstein, the baker-cum-winemaker, Schmidl, makes his speciality Wachauer *Laberl* rolls.

Austrians have known periods of great poverty this century; firstly in the wake of defeat in the First World War and subsequent depression, and secondly after the Second World War, when they were occupied by the four powers until 1955. Experiences of this sort have led them to a simple and reasonable conclusion: one should never go hungry. Wherever you go you will be offered food.

This is particularly true of wine-tastings. It is 8.30am. You have just risen from the breakfast table to get to your first tasting on time. The grower is busy pulling corks on a row of two or three dozen bottles he wants you to taste. Suddenly there is a loud clumping down the steps to the cellar: the grower's wife arrives. In her hands she is holding a bowl of snow-white lard, in the other a basket of bread. Sometimes the food is a little more sophisticated: liver paté takes the place of lard, or occasionally slices of bread and dripping sprinkled with cayenne pepper are put out to cleanse your palate between glasses.

One breakfast is rarely sufficient for an Austrian. Sometimes in the mid-morning work will grind to a halt and a *Gabelfrühstück* (fork breakfast) is dec-reed. This might take the form of a works outing to a *Würstelstand* or the *Kaffeehaus*. In the old days, however, the second breakfast was eaten at the *Beisl*:

DER PHÄAKE

Zum Gabelfrühstück gönn ich mir
Ein Tellerfleisch, ein Krügerl Bier,
Schieb an und ab ein Gollasch ein,
(Kann freilich auch ein Bruckfleisch sein),
Ein saftiges Beinfleisch, nicht zu fett,
Sonst hat man zu Mittag sein Gfrett . . .
Zur Jausen geh ich in die Stadt
Und schau, wer schöne Stelzen hat,
Ein kaltes Ganserl, jung und frisch,
Ein Alzerl Käs, ein Stückl Fisch,
Weil ich so früh am Nachmittag
Nicht schon was Warmes essen mag.

Joseph Weinheber, 1892–1945

For my fork breakfast I give myself
Boiled beef and a small jug of beer,
Rapidly engulf a goulasch,
(Or even perhaps a plate of tripe),
Or possibly a juicy stew, not too fat,
Otherwise it gives me worries around noon . . .
For a snack I go to town
To see who's got a nice pork knuckle,
Or a cold goose, young and fresh,
A bit of Alpzirler cheese, a hunk of fish;
This early in the afternoon
I can't take hot food.

These days the Viennese second breakfast is not quite so copious. It could mean a visit to Trzes-newski in the Doroteergasse or Zum Schwarzen Kameel in the Bognergasse for an open sandwich. In both places your open sandwich comes on black *Hausbrot*; in the Schwarzen Kameel, presided over by the beautiful Frau Walli, the coverings could be egg curry, red cabbage or lentils and ham. At Trzesniewski eggs predominate, blended with paprika, herrings, gherkins and the ubiquitous horseradish, or *Kren*. Frau Walli offers visitors to her *Jausenstation* (stand-up snack-bar) or to the perfect art nouveau restaurant next door, a selec-tion of wines by the glass or bottle. At Trzesnewski the customers tend to take a *Pfiff* (12.5-centilitre mug) of beer.

CAKE AND PASTRY SNACKS

In the afternoon, an alternative form of *Jause* is a sticky cake from any one of Vienna's cake and pastry shops. The most beautiful of these (despite the appalling rudeness of the staff) is Demel in the Kohlmarkt. For more than a century Demel has been fighting a battle with the Hotel Sacher over just who has the authentic recipe for the world-famous *Sachertorte*. The cake was invented by Franz Sacher, a young chef in the household of the statesman Prince Metternich in around 1835. In 1876, his son Eduard Sacher founded the insti-tution which eventually grew into the Sacher Hotel. Always available from the coffee rooms was his father's famous invention: a chocolate Savoy cake coated with apricot jam and covered with a chocolate frosting.

At Demel in the Kohlmarkt, however, Eduard Demel claimed that he had bought the true recipe from one of Franz Sacher's grandsons. The Demel version splits the sponge in two, adding a layer of apricot jam before covering it with the chocolate icing. A typically trivial Viennese controversy raged for years as to who – Demel or Sacher – possessed the true recipe. Finally, after a legal battle which also lasted for years, and certainly made the fortunes of the lawyers involved, it was

Trzesniewski in the Dorotheergasse in Vienna. Popular for snacks of open sandwiches served with a Pfiff *of beer.*

Left: Despite its unhelpful staff, Demel in the Kohlmarkt is still one of Vienna's best traiteurs.

decided that Sacher's claim was the more legitimate. Demel, however, refused to accept the court's verdict as final, and they have persisted in labelling their cake the *Ur-Sachertorte* (original *Sachertorte*).

A *Torte* is basically any round cake from which segmental slices are cut. The *Sachertorte* is by no means the only *Torte* you are likely to encounter in a coffee house or *Konditorei* (cake shop). The *Linzertorte* is almost as famous as the *Sacher*, and there is an elaborate *Esterhazy-Torte* commemorating the princely patrons of Joseph Haydn. The nut cake, or *Nusstorte*, is another hardy perennial and most Viennese cafés seem to stock a *Mohntorte* or poppy-seed cake. Recommended is the *Mohntorte* of the Café Sperl in the Gumpendorfer Strasse, as much for the taste of the cake as for elderly man-hating horse fanatic who serves it.

VORSPEISE

Most non-Austrians would not be too happy on an endless diet of sticky cakes and sausages if they thought they were going to have to sit down to a substantial lunch or dinner. If you want a proper meal selected from a wide choice of dishes enumerated on a menu, then your destination will not be the coffee house but the restaurant. A word of warning (and indeed complaint) about many Austrian restaurants, particularly provincial ones: piped music is common. Why it is believed that a perpetual battering by the flat tones of Frank Sinatra is conducive to a good appetite I cannot say, but Frank Sinatra is the number one choice in provincial Austrian restaurants.

The structure of the Austrian meal is old-fashioned; you should know in advance that most Austrians react to the word dieting with ill-concealed horror. To eat properly you should begin with a *Vorspeise*, (hors-d'oeuvre). Next comes soup and only then does one reach the main course. Some meals involve a fish or poultry course, but this only happens these days at a formal banquet or as part of a lightened *menu gastronomique*. If you are tempted by the handful of decent Austrian cheeses, these come next, and then there is the inevitable

dessert. Some Austrians like to start their meals with a glass of (often excellent) fruit schnapps. Most Anglo-Saxons will find the schnapps more pleasant at the end of the meal, when it comes in useful as a *digestif* for a fairly hefty quantity of nourishment.

A good introduction to the sheer variety of Austrian hors-d'oeuvres is provided by the restaurant Zu den Drei Husaren in Vienna's Weihburggasse. Zu den Drei Husaren was the first Viennese luxury restaurant to open after the Allied occupation, and as such it occupies a position not unlike the Tour d'Argent in Paris: respected, expensive, and largely immune to modern influences in cooking. The hors-d'oeuvres at the Drei Husaren come on four trolleys and require the services of the Old-World waiters if you want some sort of guided tour. Recently I tasted a salad of ox tongue, mini steak-tartares, Bismarck herrings and a delicious pike dumpling in a dill sauce (*Hechtknödel*).

Another speciality of Zu den Drei Husaren's trolleys is the *Kalbshirnknödel*, or veal-brains dumpling. Innards are popular with the Austrians; Reinhard Gerer, the chef at the Korso restaurant in the Bristol Hotel prepares a delicious dish of calves' lungs (*Kalbsbeuschel*) topped with a quail's egg as a *Vorspeise*. His pupil, Toni Mörwald, of the restaurant Mörwald at Feuersbrunn in Donauland-Carnuntum, has adapted the idea by adding a Riesling-based wine sauce. Mörwald is also responsible for veal tongue on a bed of red onions with the inevitable *Kren* (horseradish). Heart is also popular: Reisinger, in Pöttsching in Burgenland, mixes heart and sweetbreads in an *Einmach*. The *Einmach* is a thick, egg-yolk enriched sauce, not unlike an old-fashioned fricassee. All offal lends itself to dumplings and *Strudel* preparations, lungs and brains are often wrapped up in *Strudel*-dough and at the ultra-modern Altwienerhof in Vienna's 6th *Bezirk*, Rudi Kellner makes a sweetbread *Strudel* which he serves with scrambled quails' eggs, beetroot, tomato and capsicum. Zum Roten Wolf in Langenlebarn prepares tripe with morels in a creamy Veltliner sauce.

Now that some Austrians are rediscovering their traditional recipes (some would say that they had never lost sight of them), black pudding has become a respectable *Vorspeise* in restaurants. In the Loibnerhof, lying in the shadow of the castle where Richard the Lionheart was emprisoned, Chef Knoll deep fries his black pudding. In the earthier Birkenhof in Gols an hors-d'oeuvre of black pudding turned out to be a heaped plate, complete with fried potatoes and *Sauerkraut*, neither was the main course any more modestly garnished. Jahreszeiten in Perchtoldsdorf makes a refined version of this, putting the *Sauerkraut* into ravioli and serving it with deep-fried black pudding.

Quails are in fashion in Austria. Another new-wave Viennese restaurant is Gottfried in the 3rd *Bezirk*, where chef Josef Fadinger serves a simple roast quail's breast on a bed of curly lettuce with excellent Styrian pumpkin-seed oil. The area of Austria most famed for its poultry is Burgenland, and in Pöttsching Reisinger uses guinea fowl to good effect in a terrine with *Sauerrüben*: turnips pickled in the manner of *Sauerkraut* (sounds frightful but is actually rather good).

The Central European love affair with the pig naturally leads to a good deal of ham figuring on Austrian menus. Strange as it may seem to anyone who has visited Prague, this is often referred to as *Pragerschinken* in restaurants. Before Communism reduced Czecho-Slovakia to penury, Prague ham had a supranational reputation for quality which it does not deserve today; fortunately most *Prager-schinken* comes from Austria itself. One other ham which is worth looking out for is wild boar. In the restaurant Loibnerhof at Loiben in the Wachau, there is a good *proscuitto*-style wild boar ham.

Sucking pig is called *Spanferkel* in German. In Austria the tender young meat is sometimes used in an aspic, or *Sulz*. Again, the use of aspic has been revived of late for its ability to provide a decorative dish which can be 'plated' before the service. At the Förthof Hotel in Stein on the Danube there is a pork *Sulz* with plenty of onions. Across the river at the restaurant Schickh in Klein-Wien, the chef-proprietor uses boiled beef (*Tafelspitz*) for his *Sulz*, incorporating fresh young peas and quails' eggs within the gelatinous whole.

As in France, the prince of Austrian *Vorspeise* is foie-gras or *Ganslleber* in Austrian German. Rudi Kellner at the Altwienerhof is justly famed for his inventive use of foie gras in the kitchen. He created

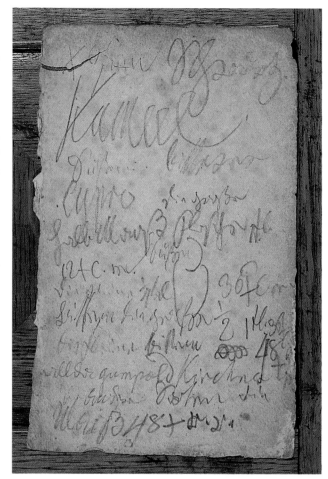

Zum Schwarzen Kameel, a Viennese stand-up snack bar cum restaurant. In the archives is this order from Beethoven.

something of a culinary joke when he used it to make a Mozart-Kugel, or Mozart bullet, in imitation of a popular Austrian chocolate. He also makes a successful pasty with foie gras, marinading the livers in Burgenland *Prädikat* wine and wrapping it in filo pastry. At the fine Barth-Stuben in Neusiedel am See, the chef serves a goose-liver *Strudel* with cabbage and a tomato sauce.

One of the most effective *Vorspeise* I tasted in Austria, however, was one of the least refined. At the restaurant Schnattl in Vienna's 8th *Bezirk*, the chef makes delicious stuffed dumplings served on a bed of onions and cabbage sweated in wine. Like so many formerly Bohemian dishes, this is one to try in Austria and not in Czecho-Slovakia; another tribute to the Austrians for their ability to lift the best from their subject nations and bring it home to

Vienna. Two decades ago I recall eating a *Risipisi*, cooked from the old Venetian recipe, in the former Jewish quarter of the Leopoldstadt: Venice too enjoyed a period under Austrian rule, and *Risipisi* (or *risi e bisi* in Venetian dialect) has long been a part of the Austrian repertoire.

As I have said, the dumpling, or *Knödel* was introduced into Austrian gastronomy by Bohemian cooks; but it should be added that the basic dumpling has undergone innumerable variations since then to become as native a part of the Austrian food world as other imports like, for example, *Wiener Schnitzel*. In the wild Waldviertel the dumplings are made from potato flour, giving them a consistency which is unlike those made from wheat flour or bread. The *Semmelknödel*, made from pounded bread rolls, is by far and away the most commonly encountered Austrian dumpling. *Serviettenknödel* comes a close second, they are made in the same way as the *Semmelknödel* but steamed in a napkin, hence the name. *Serviettenknödel* is served sliced, often with *Grammeln*. Sometimes the *Grammeln* are included in the dumplings themselves; this is the case in the Innviertel in Upper Austria, where other dumpling specialities include *Bratknödel* (similar to Schnattel's) and *Speckknödel* made with bacon fat from specially obese pigs. In the Tirol dumplings are made from bread and meat held together with an egg-yolk, while in the region of Salzburg the *Kaspressknödel* includes cheese. Elsewhere in Austria the best chefs experiment with dumplings, adding to their flavour with anything from cabbage to hogs' blood.

In the far south of Austria in Carinthia, on the borders of Yugoslavia and Italy, the speciality is *Nudeln*: large Cornish-pasty lookalikes made from pasta dough and stuffed with cheese, herbs and egg (*Kasnudeln*), or minced pork and *Grammeln* (*Fleischnudeln*). These may be found in Vienna itself, where the restaurant Bei Max in the Herrengasse specialises in Carinthian food.

Vienna has its own form of pasta, which owes little to the Italian influence present in the provinces of Carinthia and Styria. In the ordinary *Gasthaus* or *Beisl* it is possible to find a rough blend of chopped pasta and cabbage or ham called *Krautfleckerl* or *Schinkenfleckerl* (*see p* 131). Like most basic *Beisl* foods, these dishes often overdo the garlic. The Bohemian *Tascherl* is like ravioli made by an Aztec: it is three bite-sizes of potato dough made into a *roux* and enriched with an egg yolk. At the Loibnerhof in Unterloiben, Herr Knoll forgoes the potato flour to make a lighter pasta, filling the envelopes with spinach or *Grammeln*.

Sterz is rarely encountered in Vienna, but anyone wishing to visit Austria's more remote provinces should have a good idea about what it is. Sterz resembles Italian *polenta* (to the degree that it is sometimes actually called *Polenta* or *Plenten* in Carinthia or Styria). As a rule, the poorer the family, the more their diet will revolve around *Sterz*. The corn used to make the meal varies from place to place: in the Tirol both wheat and maize are used, hence the popular rhyme:

Knödl, Nudl, Muas und Plenten
Sind die vier Tiroler Elementen.

Dumplings, noodles; stewed fruit and maize meal
Are the four elements of Tirol.

In Carinthia and Styria the *Sterz* is made from maize and any made from buckwheat is called *Heidensterz* (literally, heathen meal) as a result of its strangeness to the region. In Burgenland maize-(*Kukuruz*) meal is called *Türkensterz*, because the Turks are thought to have brought maize to the area. The Burgenländers tend to make their *Sterz* from beans (*Bohnensterz*) and serve it with a bowl of bean soup; or from potatoes (*Grumbirnsterz*). Needless to say, the *Sterz* here needs a fair dollop of butter or sauce to make it palatable.

THE SOUP CULTURE

"Delicious?", said the John Cleese-like waiter in an hotel on the Danube. The Englishwoman at the next table looked embarrassed, but tried her best to manage in the circumstances.

"What's that?", she replied.

"Delicious?", the waiter repeated, pointing at the soup.

"Oh! I thought you were referring to me!", said the Englishwoman, dabbing the sides of her mouth with her napkin and heaving a sigh of relief.

One of the great joys of Austria's antediluvian gastronomic culture is that soup still plays an important role in the structure of the meal. A good soup depends on good stock and in some more sophisticated cultures the stock is used up by the chef for sauces and meat *jus*. Here in Austria, however, the soup is treated with respect and has first call on the stockpot.

Basic soup is no more than refined stock or *bouillon*, of which the most famous is the consommé or *Kraftsuppe*, to give it its German name. Clear soups are popular in Austria as they form the basis for *Einlagen*, literally what 'lies in' the broth. *Einlagen* can range from a simple *Semmelknödel* to something much more complicated like a *Lungenstrudel* (a strudel stuffed with calves' lungs). Two standard additions to clear broth are *Leberknödel* and *Griessnockerl*. *Leberknödel* are pigs'-liver dumplings often flavoured with chives; *Griessnockerl* are semolina dumplings made with two spoons, like a French *quenelle*. Another addition of the same sort is *Frittaten*: strips of chopped pancake put into the soup to render it more filling.

Potato or maize flour are the simpler ingredients used if a thicker soup is desired. Once a basic consistency is achieved with stock and potato then flavouring elements may be added. This is the idea behind the *Waldviertler Knoblauchsuppe* (Waldviertel Garlic Soup); as much garlic as the chef can find is crushed into the soup, creating havoc with your insides and causing the disaffection of your friends over a period of days. A milder Waldviertel speciality is *Rahmsuppe*, which used to be a popular standby during Lent: it is basically potato soup with soured cream. The *Kukuruzcremesuppe* found in Burgenland is the same soup made from maize. In Carinthia the potato soup is called *Kirtagssuppe* and is made with chicken stock, potatoes and caraway seeds; this bears a strong resemblance to the Styrian *Stossuppe*. Two rather grander versions on the theme of potato soup are prepared by Vienna's top restaurants: Zu den Drei Husaren, which offers a *Wiener Kartoffelsuppe* with wild mushrooms, and Rudi Kellner's version at the Altwienerhof which was quite deliciously flavourful and creamy, and very much helped by a tablespoonful of salmon eggs.

Naturally, vegetable soups, with or without cream, are also popular. A very hearty soup is the *Burgenländische Krautsuppe*. The version at the

Birkenhof Hotel in Gols in the Seewinkel is made with shredded cabbage, pork, *Debreziner* sausage and soured cream. As Gols is no more than spitting distance from Hungary, the soup also had a fair amount of paprika in it. Cabbage, cauliflower and asparagus are popular for vegetable creams. The Styrians make a cream of pumpkin soup, adding a spoonful of pumpkin-seed oil to give it flavour; in southern Burgenland bean soup is popular, creamed or otherwise.

Vegetable soups go down well in Lent, but fish soups are even better. In Stein on the Danube there is a local fish soup made with whatever can be caught from the river: pike, zander, Danube catfish and carp. The Stein soup can be rather stodgy and farinaceous; a better bet is the *Szegedi Haluszle Fischsuppe* served at the excellent Barth-Stuben in Neusiedl am See. Naturally, with a name like that it

An old restaurant sign in Vienna's 1st Bezirk.

KÜCHE

is not wholly Austrian, but it is well to remind readers that Burgenland was only detached from Hungary after the First World War. The soup is a good Balkan broth containing peppers, tomatoes, cabbage, herbs, carp and eel. The last two are from the Neusiedlersee.

A new fad in Austria is wine soup: essentially a concentrated beef or chicken stock mixed with wine and thickened with egg yolks and cream. The soup is served with croutons dipped in wine and cinnamon. The best of these that I consumed on my travels was the *Grüne Veltlinersuppe* at the Loibnerhof in Unterloiben (*see p* 130). In Styria a *Rieslingsuppe* was also good.

Naturally, the list of soups could go on forever, especially when you get to thick chicken soups like the one served in Vienna's 1900 in the Fichtegasse, or the tangy venison purée soup with game *Nockerl* created by the innovative chef at the Reisinger restaurant in Pöttsching.

One of the stars of what Austrian gastronomic writers are pleased to call their "soup culture" is Josef Fadinger at Gottfried in Vienna. A glance at a recent menu reveals a cress cream soup with a sweetbread *Strudel*; flambéed *Tafelspitz* (boiled beef) soup in an 'essence' of shallots and mushrooms; lobster ragout soup with dill and zander *Nockerl*; and poultry and asparagus cream with a ravioli of foie gras.

THE FISH COURSE

The retraction of Austria after 1918 deprived the people of its coastline. This was keenly felt by Austrians who had grown used to holidays in Dalmatia or Istria and who had known the bustle of the new port of Trieste (created in the second half of the nineteenth century on the initiative of the Rhinelander Minister of Commerce, Baron Bruck). Suddenly Austria was deprived not only of its coast and its navy, but also its fishing fleet. These days fish has to be brought in from elsewhere. Consequently it is fashionable to eat sea fish, and rich Viennese will go to extraordinary lengths to part with their money for the sake of a small chunk of sea-bass or turbot.

For those people not prepared to sell their souls for a skate or a sole, there are the river and lake fish of Austria. Despite its shallowness, the Neusiedlersee in Burgenland is well stocked with carp, pike and zander or pike-perch (Austrians sometimes use the Hungarian word *fogos* when referring to zander). Earlier this century someone had the brilliant idea of introducing Hamburg eels to the lake and they have prospered ever since. In Gols an eel was presented deep fried with a tartare sauce; under its crisp skin looking rather like a dinosaur. Carp are traditionally eaten at Christmas in Austria and South Germany. At their best they have a slightly gamey flavour; at their worst they can be muddy and oily. In the Barth-Stuben the carp was served under layers of mixed (Hungarian) vegetables and horseradish shavings. At another top Burgenland table – Reisinger – the carp had been turned into a *Sulz* (aspic) with thyme, maize, onions and gherkins in the jelly.

A speciality of the Pöttsching area is trout, farmed and fed to resemble salmon-trout. At Reisinger they are made into a creamy terrine while the Neusiedlersee zander is breadcrumbed, fried in garlic and served with *Gemüsenockerl*: finely chopped *quenelles* made from Balkan vegetables bound with egg yolk and presented on a thin *beurre blanc*.

There are quite enough trout in the mountain streams of Austria to render Schubert's sentimentality at best misplaced, at worst mawkish. In the lakes and rivers there are other coarse fish like perch, tench, gudgeon and char; while in the Danube itself there is the European cat-fish which here is called the *Wels*. Austrians are prone to tell you horror stories about the *Wels*, alleging that it can reach gigantic size in the murky, brown waters of the Danube, eat small children and occasionally threaten shipping. It does appear that they can grow to two or three metres in length, but those served in the restaurants along the river tend to measure something under a metre. The flesh of the fish is firm and gelatinous and responds well to steaming. In general the best Danube catch is the pike, which is most often fried in garlic.

Another bounty from Austria's rivers and springs used to be freshwater crayfish (*Krebs*). After the last war the starving Viennese population used to scour the Vienna Woods for crayfish and wild mushrooms as a means of staying alive. These days various plagues have decimated the crayfish population all over Europe, but I am told there is still a restaurant on the Semmering, on a stretch of Europe's most dramatic railway lines, where crayfish are served with local summer truffles. Personally, I have only ever encountered Danube crayfish in the Rossmühle restaurant in Tulln and at Mörwald in Feuersbrunn.

Naturally fish play a role in Lent. At the beginning of the fast, notices are stuck to the doors of provincial inns advertising a three day *Heringschmaus* (herring feast). The herrings are mitigated with potato and other salads. It is fairly typical of Austria that the people somehow contrive to turn a fast into a feast.

The Habsburg emperors were clearly not so keen on herrings. The story goes that they stuck to beavers and otters during Lent, having convinced themselves that anything which lived most of its life in water must necessarily be a fish. As the end approached and *Gründonnerstag* came round (Maundy Thursday), the people celebrated with spinach and eggs. Again confusion reigned: the *Grün* came from the verb *greinen*, to whine – not from the word for green. Any excuse for a blow-out.

"THE KING OF BASE BEASTS"

Nowhere is Grimod de La Reynière's description of the pig so true as in Austria: along the banks of the Danube not one iota of his porky substance is wasted. Sixty percent of Austria's meat intake is pork and it seems odd that they have allowed their native breeds to perish so utterly; Austria's most popular pig is a cross between an Austrian breed and the British Large White. The Austrians are so pleased with this half Anglo-Saxon usurper in their sties that they have baptised it *das Edelschwein* (the noble pig). Anyone who has seen to what degree pork quality can decline through unrestricted use of geometric carcass animals like the Large White is likely to be of another opinion, and will probably think it more of a *Pöbelschwein* (plebeian pig). In Britain we are labouring to recreate the porcine population which used to inhabit this island. When we have achieved some level of success perhaps the Austrians will be interested in trying one or two other British pigs.

Austrian pig-fancying can be a consuming passion. In Mörbisch on the Neusiedlersee I was introduced to a grower who was particularly anxious that we should try his black pudding, or *Blunz'n* as they call it in Burgenland. It was a good, creamy pudding, made from white bread, pork skin, *Grammeln*, back fat, marjoram and spices. The blood was very fresh. As I was told, only after eating liberal quantities, the pig had been killed only an hour before. Ignoring any pallor which might have appeared on the face of his English guest, the Burgenländer proceeded to give a full account of what he intended to do with his freshly slaughtered hog. The dark meat was going to make *Schubwurst*, along with more *Grammeln*, the spleen, the skin, caraway and spices; the whole then being shoved (*schieben*) into a runner.

My host was particularly anxious to recoup the lard. Lard is the foundation stone of Austrian cooking. Austrians go to great lengths to ensure that their lard is as white and neutral as possible, as they are quite likely to deep fry doughnuts and other sweet things in it. The lard is distilled from the back fat, chopped fine and mixed with water. More sausages came next on the Burgenländer's list of priorities: *Bratwurst*, *Presswurst* and *Schwartl-magen*, the latter a sort of Austrian haggis made from the pig's stomach. Then came the hams and the pork *Schnitzels*. The man from Mörbisch had planned to tuck into the *Schnitzels* that evening. The *Schweinsbraten* (roasting meat), was to be set aside for later in the week while the liver, fried with onions, was destined for the morning breakfast table.

The remoter the part of Austria, the more obsessed the people appear to be with the variety of uses they have for their pig. Willi Sattler, the star winemaker from Gamlitz in South Styria, who also owns the Sattlerhof restaurant, explains a plateful of cold cuts with loving detail: here was the seasoned pigs' skin or *Schwarten*; this was *Verhackertes* or chopped *Speck*; this corner of the plate contained *Selchfleisch*, lightly smoked flesh from the upper thigh; and this *Selchwurst*, or smoked sausage.

The obsession is justified by lengthy tradition: pork is, after all, the most convenient of meats. Processed, it can be used in a hundred different ways: hence the parties which followed the killing of the beast. Philippina Welser, the morganatic wife of a sixteenth-century Habsburg duke, listed 30 recipes for pork. Anyone wanting to try a large number of these preparations should try the *Bauernschmaus* (literally peasant's feast), which contains at least half a dozen different porky derivatives. More far-reaching interpretations may be had from a *Heurige* or *Buschenschank*. Here you will see tables piled high with all forms of smoked ham and ribs, slicing sausage, juicy cooked sausage, coils of black pudding and hunks of roasting meat. At

An Austrian farmer with his pride and joy.

Christmas, some families forgo the traditional goose in favour of smoked pork (*Geselchtes*) which is, after all, more of a tribute to the animal that has sustained them throughout the year. After *Wiener Schnitzel*, Austria's second-favourite Sunday lunch is a *Schweinsrostbraten* (roast pork).

Some provincial restaurants advertise *Stelzen*-days. A *Stelze* is what the South Germans call a *Schweinshaxe* and the Prussians call an *Eisbein*; in England we call it a pork knuckle and we eat it but rarely. On a knuckle-day you can eat as many knuckles as takes your fancy.

Pork knuckles are popular in the Weinviertel where another pork dish is *Sauerbraten*, in which the joint is left in brine for two weeks. It should be unnecessary to add here that, being so close to the Waldviertel, the people believe in stuffing the meat with a great deal of garlic. Elsewhere in the region I have seen pork fillet served under a thick crust of caraway and breadcrumbs. In the Weinviertel I also saw a pork dish with the curious name of *Jungfernspeise* (virgin's treat). Naturally, there was some interest in what exactly virgins eat in the Weinviertel: in fact it was pork fillet wrapped in smoked bacon.

The Hungarian influence is once again uppermost when it comes to Burgenland pork specialities. In the highly-rated but physically hideous restaurant G'würzstöckl, in Eisenstadt's Hotel Burgenland, the chef prepares *Szegediner Kraut-fleisch* in which pork fillet is served pink on a bed of tomatoes, cabbage and paprika. Other Burgenland

*A huge selection of sausages in the bleak, modern Land-
strasse Markt in Vienna. Austrians use every part of the pig.*

pork dishes influenced by Hungarian food include
the *Schindlbraten*, in which pork is served highly
spiced with capsicum, and *Kotelett Bakony* (pork
chops in a mild, creamy paprika sauce).

In Styria the pork is often boiled, as in the
Steierisches Wurzelfleisch eaten in the Rebenhof
Hotel in Ratsch. The pork arrived with quantities
of root vegetables cooked with it and with shavings
of the ever-present horseradish. An oddity encountered in Styria but apparently without any specific
territorial validity is the *Falsche Forelle*. This 'false
trout' might have proved a boon to Franz Schubert;
as its name implies, it contains no trout at all. The
'trout' is actually a pancake containing minced pork
and marjoram which is covered in breadcrumbs
and deep fried. By some happy accident the winemaking Polz family of Spielfeld chose to serve this
pancake on Shrove Tuesday.

One more curiosity of the Austrian pork repertoire is the favourite dish of Vienna's charismatic
anti-Semitic mayor, Karl Lueger (1844–1910).
Lueger is chiefly remembered outside Austria for
having delivered the memorable line "*I sog' wer a
Jud' is*", (I decide who's a Jew). In Austria itself his
achievement is believed to be more positive and he
still merits an important *Platz* and statue on the
inner-city *Ring*. His pork was a fillet, split and
flattened, seasoned, dipped in oil and breadcrumbs,
baked and served with a *Béarnaise* sauce and *maître
d'hotel* butter. The mayor liked his pork with chips
and his recipe may be sampled at the Reisner
restaurant in Forchtenstein in Burgenland.

BEEF, VEAL, LAMB AND MUTTON

A quarter of the Austrians' meat intake is beef.
Their fondness for the ox goes back almost as far as
their affection for pigs. In 1793, the Prussian writer
Friedrich Nicolai estimated that the Viennese ate
25 percent more beef than the Londoners "who eat

virtually nothing else''. Most of these cattle came from Hungary. Today many Austrians have become keen on steak, and restaurants like Zur Schönen Aussicht in Vienna's 9th *Bezirk* specialise in cuts which can be pushed quickly under the grill. Traditionally, however, boiled meat plays an important part in Austria's beef culture, and the most famous boiled beef dish is *Tafelspitz*. *Tafelspitz* is silverside boiled in beef broth and, (when the meat is half cooked), root vegetables and herbs are added (*see p 132*). The meat is cut into thick slices, moistened with the broth and strewn with chopped chives. Like a French *pot-au-feu*, it is served with chopped gherkins and rock salt. Naturally, horseradish is also served; often as *Apfelkren* in which the root is blended with apple purée. *Tafelspitz* may be obtained virtually anywhere in Vienna or Lower Austria.

There are a number of other boiled beef cuts popular in Austria; one of special note is the *Fledermaus* (bat): you've seen the Johann Strauss operetta – now eat the cast.

Roast meat often pays lip-service to the great noble families of the Austrian court in whose honour dishes were created. A popular beef dish is the *Esterházy-Rindsbraten* with a garnish of root vegetables and capers braised in butter and lemon juice. Another dish commemorates the noble Trautmansdorff family: the meat is braised with truffles, mushrooms and vegetables and served with baked tomatoes, puréed potatoes and small gherkins. In Burgenland you will find the *Zigeunerrostbraten* or gypsy's roast; naturally this comes with a paprika sauce as well as a deal of smoked bacon. Lastly, a *Zwiebelrostbraten* is another popular dish in Lower Austria; as its name implies it comes with a thick onion sauce.

The last decades of the Habsburg Empire introduced a *modus vivendi* which united the Emperor's Austrian and Hungarian subjects. The Magyars ceased resisting the Austrians and set about trying to prevent power from getting into the hands of the Empire's large Slavic population. During this time most Magyar dishes were assimilated into the Viennese repertory. The best-known of these was undoubtedly *Gulasch* which requires a careful attention to onions, garlic, tomatoes and above all paprika. Paprika is strictly graded in Viennese markets and shops, so that the right strength is used to prepare the proper dish. One restaurant which tries to recreate dishes from the turn of the century is 1900 in the Fichtegasse. 1900 offers a very good *Filetspitzengulasch* made from the best (*Spitzen*) of the fillet.

Only ten percent of the Austrians' meat-intake is veal, but veal is honoured in their favourite dish, the *Wiener Schnitzel*. In general it must be true to say that veal accounts for more of the meat consumed at good restaurant tables than either pork or beef. It has often been said that the most famous item in the Viennese gastronomy was nothing more than an import from Milan, where the *Costoletta alla Milanese* had been in vogue since Renaissance times. The *Wiener Schnitzel*, it turns out, was one of the spoils of war: Marshal Radetzky introduced it to the Viennese court having successfully crushed the revolution of 1848 in Milan. The Viennese, however, made a considerable number of adaptations to the Lombard dish (were they not also Lombards?); as experts on breadcrumbs they substituted pounded rolls for white bread, to make the *Schnitzel* crunchier. Above all, they rejected the cutlet in favour of the escalope.

Schnitzel, made from either veal or pork, is still the favourite for Sunday lunch; eaten either hot or cold with potato salad (*Erdäpfelsalat*). Apart from *Schnitzel*, veal is roasted with *Speck* and paprika or with a *Semmel* or spinach stuffing. Prince Metternich had a suitably superb recipe for a saddle of veal which involved truffle slices and a paprika-enriched *béchamel* squashed between each thick slice. In Burgenland there is a popular veal gulasch called *Pörkölt*. The calves' insides are also popular and Vienna's Korso restaurant prepares a simple but effective recipe for liver with cabbage and butter.

Until Austrian cooks began to take stock of what was popular in Western Europe, the eating of lamb was confined to Easter Sunday. Now lamb, cooked pink – French-style – is a speciality of up-market restaurants, and the seasonings, which involve rosemary, thyme or pink or green peppercorns, are also gastronomic imports. Sheep are farmed in the south of the country, especially in Carinthia and Styria, and it is to those regions that one must look for authentically Austrian recipes. The best known is the Styrian mutton dish *Steirisches Schöpsernes*. The mutton is braised in water, root vegetables, herbs and potatoes, then buried under horseradish shavings before serving.

POULTRY AND GAME

Naturally, poultry is also popular in Austria. In the modern Landstrasse Markt in Vienna one is struck by the intense yellow colouring of the chickens which hang above the stalls: a sign either that they are properly fed on a maize diet or that they have been tampered with in some way. Let us hope it is the former. Baked chicken in breadcrumbs (*Wiener Backhendl*) is one of the most popular dishes in the Lower Austrian *Gasthaus* or *Beisl*. More important than chicken is the fondness for other farmyard poultry such as geese and ducks. The goose is the favourite Christmas dish and it is also traditionally served on Martinmass (11 November) with a compliment of stuffed apricots. Duck is valued for its breast; in Donauland-Carnuntum, Toni Mörwald serves his in a crunchy-outside, pink-inside new-wave style. Reisinger in Burgenland offered his farmhouse duck breast with a potato *Strudel* flavoured with bacon fat.

With so much of the country covered with mountains and forest, game is abundant. The shooting season is possibly the best time to visit Austria, while the pre-Lenten balls rage in Vienna and the best game is hanging up above the stalls of the Landstrassemarkt and the Naschmarkt. Anyone wishing to be reminded of what is in season can take a short walk from the Staatsoper and see the long lines of chamois, wild boar, roe and fallow deer, hare, pheasant and partridge. Sometimes the stallholders wrap the game birds in little parcels of *Speck* for a particularly succulent roasting.

Clearly the top restaurants handle game the best. Out in the local provincial *Gasthaus* game can be disappointing: the meat so overcooked that it flakes under the fork, while in a lumpy gravy floats an incongruous-looking slice of orange on which has been dropped a spoonful of cranberry jelly. One country restaurant, not far from the capital, managed to render a simple dish of red deer totally tasteless; something which made me all the more angry when I emerged from lunch to be greeted by the steady gaze of a troop of the animal's brothers,

A stall in the Naschmarkt. This central street market is transformed on Saturdays when Austrian farmers sell their produce directly to the Viennese.

all looking in the best of health.

On the more positive side, restaurants such as Steirereck in Vienna have no problems knowing how to cook venison. The restaurant Korso served roe deer *noisettes* with red cabbage. At the Altwienerhof they served the saddle, nicely tender and not overcooked. A little further down the price scale comes Schnattl who offers well-cooked strips of roe deer on a bed of horn-of-plenty mushrooms. At Gottfried there were cutlets hewn from the *Frischling* (young wild boar).

Olives sold in the Naschmarkt. Many of the stalls are now operated by Turks and Serbians.

THE CHEESE-BOARD

Looking at the Austrian countryside with its lush pastures, deep meadows and happy, browsing Alpine cattle (with or without Julie Andrews) one might easily leap to conclude that this country, like neighbouring Switzerland, is a paradise for cheese-lovers. Sadly, this is not quite the case. Foolish government policy seems to go some way towards explaining the lack of decent cheese and why those who can afford to, and almost all the better restaurants, buy only imported cheese. Firstly, the post-war socialist régimes were at pains to have all Austrian milk brought to the cooperative dairies which exercised a virtual monopoly on cheese and butter production. Secondly, the Austrian mania for having all food products clean to the point of sterilisation has meant that, until now, all soft cheeses have had to be made from pasteurised milk and stored in such a way as to inhibit all chance of maturation. Hard cheeses have fared a little better and one or two have the sort of acid tang which betrays the farmer's continued use of proper, raw milk.

A cheese tasting, specially organised at the restaurant Steirereck, proved something of a disappointment, despite the ministrations of both the highly talented waiters who keep the keys to the wine cellar and the cheese room respectively. Most of the cheeses shown were profoundly imitative and not up to the standard of their models: *Österzola*, for example, is a fairly lame Gorgonzola lookalike; *Weisser Prinz* is a ewes'-milk Brie made from pasteurised milk and lacking in bite; *Geisberger* is a bland goats'-milk Camembert; *Alpzirler* is a Tilsit-style cheese, but quite fruity despite its use of pasteurised milk; there are no prizes for guessing the role-model for *Dolce Bianca*. The blue *Trauten-felser Edelschimmel* is a reasonably successful Roquefort lookalike; and Austrian Parmesan, despite the honesty of its name and the attempts the producers make to give it the taste of the original, is rubbery and lacking in the salt crystals which make the Parma cheese so great. The best of the purely imitative cheeses tasted that afternoon was the *Gaishorner Emmental Auslese* which was made from raw milk and matured for six months.

A good selection of Austrian goats' cheeses. Post war Austrian cheeses were among the dullest in Europe, but there are signs of recovery.

The rest of the tasting might be divided up between the commercial luncheon-cheese styles and Austria's few claims to fame in the cheese line. A pure luncheon style was the *Steirischer Alm-frischkäse* which, but for its pyramid form, might have been the terrible French *Roulé*; *Raffinesse* was another forgettable cheese, creamy enough but of overwhelming blandness; *Sankt Patron* was slightly richer but without bite; the same was true of *Mondseer* from Upper Austria. The best of this flight was, in my opinion, the ewes' milk-dominated *Steirischer Selchkas*; this smoked cheese would make a good companion for a glass of Bass brown ale.

Now the dinner cheeses: one which generally merits very positive remarks in Austria is the *Murecker Butterkäse* from Styria. Possibly I have never tasted this at its best, for there has always been something rather rubbery about it. Better by far, and possibly the top Austrian soft cheese in mass distribution, is the *Graf Görz* from Lienz in the Eastern Tyrol. At its best this cheese can have the consistency of a decent *Chaource* and is a good counterpoint to the better red wines of Burgenland. Another cheese with an extensive public is the *Südsteirischer Hauerkäse*. Despite its use of pasteurised milk, it achieves better acidity by being coated in wine lees from the oenological school at Silberberg in Styria. A raw-milk cheese is the *Zillertaler* from the Tirol. Aged for six months, the *Zillertaler* is strong-flavoured. A true washed-rind cheese with the pungency associated with the style is the *Achleitner Schlosskäse*; it has a slightly dusty taste, but is not disagreeable. *Ziegett* is a cows'-milk/goats'-milk blend from Salzburg which has a good balance between cream and bite. Finally, *Ennstaler* is another blue cheese made from 60 percent ewes' milk. Again the balance is good and the ewes' milk adds something of a nutty character to the blend.

At the end of the tasting the cheese waiter brought out some *rarissime* farmhouse cheeses. In recent years there has been a move towards more natural methods of cheese-making among young Austrians and a few of them have begun experimenting. This has occurred most of all in the wild Waldviertel and in Styria.

After a rather bitter little goat from the Tyrol, we had two first-rate cheeses from the Waldviertel: a 'Camembert' (goat) which was ripe and runny and very well made; and another soft goat with a pleasantly long acidity. The very last cheese was a successful ewes' milk cheese from Voitszburg in Styria. Let us hope that the future lies in cheeses like these. Sadly, very few of the others do anything like justice to the landscape.

THE DESSERT COURSE

Many might complain about the dullness of the cheeses, few would say the same about Austrian desserts. In provincial restaurants on Sundays it is not rare to see old ladies come in to take a bowl of soup and follow it up with some massive pudding. Who could blame them? They are selecting from two of the best elements of the menu. *All* Czechs and even quite a few Austrians maintain that any number of the famous Austrian desserts are Bohemian in origin and one or two Hungarian. Either way, Austria is an excellent place to sample them.

The most famous of all Austrian puddings is the *Apfelstrudel*, and here the borrowing is not from Austria's neighbours, but probably from their old enemies the Turks. From the beginning the *Strudel* dough has never been reserved just for apples; anything could then, and now, be transformed into a *Strudel*: almonds, curd cheese (*Topfen*), cream, cabbage, poppy seeds, nuts, herbs, meat, crayfish, potatoes, plums, cherries, pears, apricots, ham, Parmesan cheese, *Semmel* and cinnamon. The important thing in all these *Strudel* is to get the flakey, crispy dough just right.

Apfelstrudel may be found in virtually every coffee house and most of the *Beisln* of Vienna. Next to the apple version, the most popular today is that made from *Topfen* or, as the Germans call it, *Quark*. In general, the *Topfenstrudel* contains raisins and is served with a vanilla custard.

As we have seen, *Palatschinken* were culled from Hungary. These are also stuffed with *Topfen* on occasion and then baked in the oven. The more usual form of serving *Palatschinken* for dessert, however, is with whipped cream and apricot jam (*Marillenmarmelade*). I have occasionally come across *Mohnpalatschinken*; these contain the ubiquitous poppy-seeds.

The best way to consume poppy-seeds is in the Waldviertler dish, *Mohnnudeln*: but once again a word of warning is necessary. Outside the region Austrians ascribe the dopey nature of the Waldvierteler to an excessive consumption of poppy-seeds. Apparently the seeds have a slight narcotic effect, which is why they are put in napkins and given to teething children. Beware: do not drive after *Mohnnudeln*. The *Nudel* has nothing to do with the English noodle. The pudding *Nudel* is a fat, long dumpling; generally made from potato flour. You may eat good *Mohnnudeln* at Korso-bei-der-Oper in fashionable Vienna, but the best *Mohnnudeln* I had while researching this book were to be found at the Stadthotel in Eggenburg in the Weinviertel. They were far from prepossessing to look at; like a lot of maggots lying under the contents of an upturned ash-tray; but they were quite delicious.

Another element of Austrian cooking which may be either sweet or savoury is the *Knödel*. One favourite form of sweet *Knödel* is to make them from breadcrumbs, putting the fruit into the hollow insides. Apricot is the fruit most frequently used in this sort of recipe, but apples, pears, cherries or pineapple may also be used. Another popular form of sweet *Knödel* is made from *Topfen* covered with breadcrumbs and sugar. *Topfenknödel* are almost invariably married to *Zwetschken* or *Marillenröster*: plum or apricot compôte.

Krapfen are doughnuts or fritters; although it is as well to note that savoury versions are not unusual here either. *Faschingskrapfen* are a great feature of Austrian life in the pre-Lenten weeks. Every coffee house and every *Konditorei* must offer these carnival doughnuts filled with apricot jam. The carnival is taken very seriously in Catholic Austria, with the best Viennese balls taking place in the weeks between Christmas and the beginning of Lent. Even in little villages in the wilds of beyond the people celebrate the end of the carnival with a ball, perhaps in the local schoolhouse. While these highjinks are taking place, the villagers munch through huge piles of *Faschingskrapfen*. Another form of *Krapfen* – *Brandteigkrapferl* – is no more than a vast profiterole.

Buchteln or *Wuchteln* (from the Czech *buchtǐcky*) are jam-filled dumplings which have been adopted by Austrians everywhere. In the Waldviertel they call them *Baudexen* and in Burgenland *Beugel*. Like other sweet dumplings, their filling is their main claim to fame. In this case *Powidl* is the traditional Viennese favourite: plum compôte (generally highly spiced with cinnamon and mace). In Burgenland the *Beugel* are scattered with nuts.

Kaiserschmarren is a simple pancake reduced to atomic form as if by being scrambled in the pan. As with all dishes prefaced with the Kaiser's name, this *Schmarren* comes from the heart of Austrian bourgeois cooking and alludes to the bourgeois *Kaiser* Franz-Joseph. The use of the Imperial designation is a good example of the practice of ironic self-deprecation which the Austrians call *Schmäh*. The *Kaiserschmarren* is considered by many to be the king of Austrian puddings; a creamy pancake broken into bite-sized pieces, strewn with raisins and dusted with icing sugar.

Of course, there are many more Austrian puddings and a whole book would be needed to describe adequately the many different *Schnitten*, (fruit or chocolate slices), *Auflauf* (pudding cooked in a bain-marie) or *Weinbrot* (dry bread revived with wine and sugar and served during the vintage). Visitors should not, however, leave Austria without experiencing something made with elderberries. Austrians make a special effort to use this fruit to advantage while we try our best to leave it to fester on the tree. In one such recipe the highly scented flowers are dipped in butter and deep fried, while the berries are used as fillings for *Krapfen*. The best use of elderberries I met with was in the restaurant Reisinger in Pöttsching in Burgenland; this was the *Griesflammerie*: a mixture of elderberries, *Topfen* and semolina which had the appearance of caviar and a wonderfully crunchy, fruity consistency.

THE DIGESTIF

It would be a mistake to rise from an Austrian dinner table without calling for a small glass of schnapps. Put out of your head the fiery, raw mixtures of rocket fuel and gin you have encountered in Germany and Northern Europe, Austrian schnapps ranges from a grappa style which can rival anything you may have tasted in Italy, to a dry fruit liqueur which you might have tasted in Alsace, the Black Forest or Switzerland; in none of these places, however, is it likely to be as good as that from any half-decent Austrian restaurant.

Of course there is *bad* schnapps and it can be found all over Austria. In old Vienna there used to be bars called *Branntweiner* (literally brandies) where wizened old men and women spent the day tippling rough schnapps. There are still one or two left, notably in the now gentrified Josefstadt. The most popular shot here is called an *Obstler*, a crude distillate made from windfall apples and pears.

The quality factor behind Austrian schnapps seems to be the very limited governmental interference. In France, spirit distilling has been hit by the abolition of the old hereditary distilling rights of the *bouilleurs de crus*. In Italy the marc for grappa has to be shipped hundreds of miles before it can be distilled; but in Austria many winemakers and fruit farmers still enjoy the right to make their liqueurs on the premises. The result is obviously fresher fruit and more lively nuances in the glass.

Fruit schnapps is the kind most commonly found in restaurants. Generally the establishment goes to some trouble to make sure that they have decent stuff, and the rule is: the better the restaurant the more likely it is that the schnapps will be good. In the Birkenhof Hotel in Gols in Burgenland, the schnapps came in a small, lidded glass; the theory being that all the aromas should be kept in. Every known fruit is rendered into schnapps in Austria. Many are unexpected. Juniper schnapps, for example, is a much more welcome late-evening drop than gin; elderberries provide aromas which grandmother never dreamed of getting into her homemade wine. Rowan berries are the source for one of the best and rarest; and the rarest of all is that made from the *Els* or *Adlitzbeere*. Dictionaries are silent as to its identity; all that I can say is that its berries come from a tree which takes 15 years to fruit and that it is very expensive.

I had it for the first time in the Steirereck restaurant in Vienna, and was able to observe that the berry had a very pronounced smell of marzipan. Months later, in the Altwienerhof restaurant in the same city, the *sommelier* set down a trio of schnappses for the English table and waited to see if the foreigners could identify them. The first was a *Ringlottenbrand* (greengages), the second a *Quittenbrand* (quinces) and the third was our old friend the *Adlitzbeere*. The waiter gawped while the tasting panel went to work, and at the final pronouncement took to his heels, disappearing through the doors into the kitchen. A few minutes later there came the portly figure of the chef, Rudi Kellner: "Where is the English person", he barked, "who recognised the *Adlitzbeere* . . .?"

Right: Café Landtmann draws clientele from the Burgtheater, the Parliament and the University.

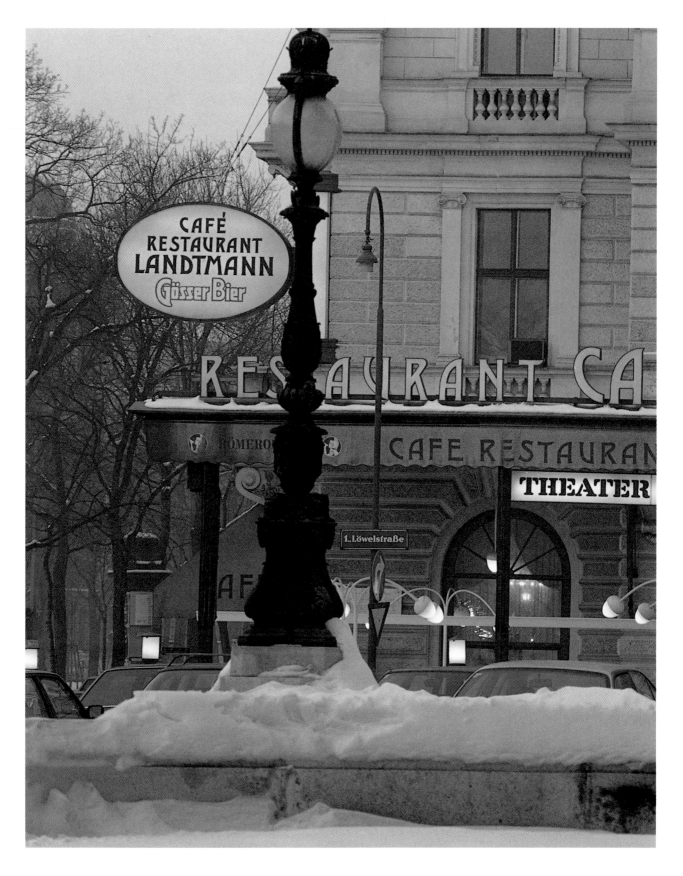

RECIPES FROM AUSTRIAN RESTAURANTS

All the recipes are for four people.

WACHAUER VELTLINERSUPPE
(*Wachau Veltliner Soup*)

These simple wine soups can now be found in any number of decent Austrian restaurants. They are easy to make and generally I have found them delicious. This recipe comes from the Loibnerhof restaurant.

7 oz/200 g puff pastry
1 egg, beaten
¾ pt/425 ml dry Veltliner wine
1½ pt/850 ml chicken stock
small stick of cinnamon
1 tsp potato starch
4 egg yolks
4 tbsp double cream
extra ground cinnamon for decoration

Roll out the pastry on a lightly floured board and cut into 6 triangles. Roll up from the long side to the point, then bend into crescent shape. Brush with beaten egg and chill for 30 minutes. Bake at Gas 6 400°F (200°C) for 10 minutes, or until risen and golden. Transfer to a wire rack to cool.

In a pan bring the wine and stock, with a cinnamon stick, to the boil and reduce by a third. Remove from the heat and cool slightly. Remove the cinnamon stick. Mix the potato starch with the egg yolks and cream. Whisk the reduced broth mixture into the egg yolk mix. Return to the pan.

Stir constantly over a gentle heat to thicken, taking care not to allow the mixture to boil, otherwise it will curdle. Pour into warmed bowls and sprinkle with cinnamon. Serve with puff pastry *stangln* (crescents).

OCHSENSCHLEPPTARTELETT AUF WEISSER ZWIEBELVINAIGRETTE
(*Oxtail Tarts with White Onion Vinaigrette*)

This recipe, from the hotel-restaurant Vier Jahreszeiten in Vienna, requires cooked oxtail and it should be remembered that this needs long and slow cooking in order to make it tender.

1 carrot, peeled
½ turnip, peeled
2 sticks of celery
3 tbsp oil
2 oz/50 g red lentils
2 oz/50 g brown lentils
1 tbsp white wine vinegar
zest of ½ orange
salt and freshly ground black pepper
8 slices of ham
1 lb/450 g cooked oxtail, stripped from the bone
2 tbsp pumpkin oil
grated horseradish, snipped chives for decoration

for the vinaigrette
1 small onion, peeled and grated
1 tbsp cider vinegar
4 tbsp sunflower oil
salt and freshly ground black pepper

Cut the vegetables into tiny dice, then toss quickly in oil in a small pan until cooked but still crunchy. Reserve.

Cook the lentils in boiling water until tender. Drain and rinse in cold water. Stir them into the vegetable dice. Season with vinegar, orange zest, salt and freshly ground black pepper.

Line a 4 in/10 cm tartlet tin with clingfilm. Add a slice of ham. Mix the oxtail with the vegetable and lentil mix and spoon on top. Place another slice of ham on top. Cover with a baking sheet and weigh it down. Leave for 30 minutes.

Carefully invert to turn out the tartlets onto a baking sheet and peel off film. Sprinkle with pumpkin oil and heat under a grill.

Shake the vinaigrette ingredients in a screwtop jar and pour onto 4 plates. Place a tartlet on top.

Decorate with the chives and coarse grated curls of horseradish.

◆

KRAUTWICKLER VOM WALLER AUF RIESLINGSAUCE
(Cabbage and Catfish Roll with Riesling Sauce)

Catfish is plentiful in the US but, apart from Telford in Shropshire, rare in the UK. Sole would be perfect for this recipe from the restaurant Gasthof Schafelner in Haag-Stadt.

12 oz/350 g catfish, skinned and boned
8 cabbage leaves, blanched

for the stuffing
5 oz/150 g catfish trimmings in small pieces
2 slices of white bread, crusts removed
½ oz/15 g butter
1 egg
2 tbsp double cream
salt and freshly ground black pepper

for the sauce
4 fl oz/100 ml fish stock
4 fl oz/100 ml Riesling
½ oz/15 g butter
2 fl oz/50 ml double cream

Place the stuffing ingredients in a food processor and blend well.

Chop the catfish fillets and mix with the stuffing. Lay 8 small squares of clean muslin on a worktop and place a cabbage leaf on each. Spoon a little stuffing mix on top. Roll up and secure with cocktail sticks. Poach for 15 minutes.

For the sauce, pour the stock into a pan and add the Riesling. Bring to the boil and reduce by half. Whisk in butter, cream and seasoning. Remove the rolls from poaching water and remove the muslin. Arrange on individual plates and drizzle over the sauce to serve.

ZANDER MIT ROTEN RÜBENSTREIFEN UND KRENOBERSSAUCE
(Zander with Beetroot Strips and Creamed Horseradish Sauce)

Zander may be ordered from a top fishmonger. Otherwise use pike for this recipe which comes from the Landhaus-Bacher restaurant in Mautern.

for the beetroot
2 medium beetroots, peeled
1 tsp caraway seeds
2 fl oz/50 ml vegetable stock
dash of sherry vinegar
salt and freshly ground black pepper
1 oz/25 g chilled butter, in pieces

for the fish
8 fillets of zander or pike
6 tbsp fresh white breadcrumbs
2 oz/50 g butter

for the horseradish sauce
¼ pt/150 ml fish stock
¼ pt/150 ml double cream
2 egg yolks
freshly grated horseradish to taste

Cook the beetroot in boiling salted water with the caraway seeds until tender but with a crisp bite. Cut into strips. Place in a pan with the stock, sherry vinegar and seasoning. Bring to the boil and stir in the butter. Remove from heat and reserve.

Season fish fillets and dredge with breadcrumbs. Melt the butter in a pan and fry fish until cooked through, turning once. Remove and keep hot.

For the horseradish sauce, heat the fish stock to bubbling point in a pan. Remove from the heat and whisk in the cream and egg yolks. Return to a low heat whisking continuously until slightly thickened. Do not allow the sauce to boil, or it will curdle. Stir in the horseradish.

Pour the sauce onto serving plates. Arrange the fish on top and decorate with the beetroot strips.

◆

GEKOCHTER TAFELSPITZ
(*Boiled Silverside*)

This is the Austrian equivalent to the French *Pot au Feu* in a recipe donated by Zu den drei Husaren, Vienna's most luxurious restaurant.

2 lb/900 g silverside
2 onions, skin on, halved
2 large carrots, peeled and in chunks
2 sticks of celery, chopped
1 leek, cleaned and chopped
10 peppercorns
2 sprigs parsley
salt
8 slices beef marrow
1 tsp fresh snipped chives

Bring a pan of water to the boil and add the silverside. Turn the heat down to simmer.

Halve the onions and scorch in a pan without fat until brown. Add them to the beef and then add the carrot, celery and leek, peppercorns, parsley and salt. Continue cooking until beef is tender.

Remove the onion from the stock and discard. Strain the vegetables and place in a warmed serving dish, reserving the stock. Add the marrow to the hot stock and pour into a tureen. Carve the meat and arrange on a platter. Serve the soup and marrow with the vegetables in a separate dish.

Sprinkle with chives.

---◆---

KALBSVÖGERL IN RIESLINGSAUCE AUF GEMÜSESTREIFEN
(*Veal Olives in Riesling Sauce*)

A good recipe from Zum Roten Wolf, one of Austria's most exciting kitchens.

1 veal knuckle, boned and trimmed
seasoned flour
4 tbsp oil
½ bottle Riesling
½ pt/300 ml veal stock
4 tbsp double cream

1 oz/25 g chilled butter in pieces
2 oz/50 g butter
salt and freshly ground black pepper
1 large carrot, peeled and in matchsticks
2 sticks celery in strips
1 courgette in strips
1 leek, cleaned and in strips

Cut the veal knuckle vertically into four. Dip into the seasoned flour. Heat the oil in a pan and brown the veal on all sides. Pour the wine over and add the stock. Bring to the boil and simmer until tender. Remove the veal and keep hot.

Add the cream to the cooking juices and whisk in the chilled butter in pieces. Season. In a separate pan, melt the butter and gently cook the vegetables until just softened. Arrange on plates with the veal. Pour the sauce over and serve with rice or noodles.

---◆---

KRAUTFLECKERL
(*Viennese Pasta and Cabbage*)

A good everyday dish often encountered in the more traditional Viennese *Beisl*. Ham is frequently substituted for the shredded cabbage. This recipe comes from Vienna's restaurant 1900.

½ white cabbage, finely shredded
salt and freshly ground black pepper
1 oz/25 g butter
1 oz/25 g dripping
1 large onion, peeled and finely chopped
1 tsp caraway seeds
3 cloves garlic, peeled and crushed
12 oz/350 g noodles

Season the cabbage by working in the salt and pepper by hand.

Melt the butter and dripping in the pan. Add the onion and cook over a gentle heat to soften. Stir in the cabbage, caraway and garlic. Cook until browned, stirring continuously.

Cook the pasta in lightly salted boiling water until *al dente*. Drain and mix into the cabbage mixture to serve.

STEINPILZE UND MANGOLD MIT WILDENTENBRUST
(*Ceps with Mangelwurzel and Wild Duck Breast*)

Helmut Österreicher, the chef at the restaurant Steirereck, proposes this daring combination of ceps and mangelwurzel with duck breast. If you cannot find mangelwurzel, swedes would be a perfectly acceptable alternative.

4 duck breasts
salt and freshly ground black pepper
1 tbsp freshly chopped mixed herbs
1 tbsp duck fat
2 oz/50 g *speck*, chopped
1 bayleaf
8 juniper berries
½ pt/300 ml game stock
1 mangelwurzel, trimmed and chopped
cep-flavoured olive oil
½ tsp caraway seeds
4 ceps, wiped

for the Hollandaise
3 tbsp white wine vinegar
1 shallot, peeled and finely chopped
4 black peppercorns
2 egg yolks
½ pt/300 ml melted clarified butter
cep-flavoured olive oil

Trim the duck breast and season with salt and freshly ground black pepper. Sprinkle over herbs. Cook both sides, skin side down first, in a little fat to brown.

Add the *speck*, bayleaf, juniper berries and continue to cook until duck breasts are browned but still pink in the centre. Remove and keep hot. Add the game stock to the pan juices and bring to the boil. Reduce and strain. Reserve.

Blanch the mangelwurzel in boiling salted water until just tender. Drain and dress in the cep oil. Season with salt and freshly ground black pepper.

Cut the ceps into thick strips and fry in cep oil with the caraway seeds.

To make the Hollandaise, in a small pan reduce the vinegar with the shallot and peppercorns until a tbsp remains. Take the pan off the heat and add the egg yolks and whisk until creamy. Gradually whisk in the butter drop by drop until the mixture thickens. Continue whisking in the butter in a thin stream until all is incorporated. Cool and stir in a few drops of cep oil.

Mix the ceps and mangelwurzel and pour the Hollandaise over. Grill to brown. Serve with duck breasts and sauce.

◆

REHMEDAILLONS MIT BURGUNDERSAUCE
(*Venison Medallions with Burgundy Sauce*)

This recipe comes from one of the prettiest restaurants in the historic centre of Vienna. The Konig von Ungarn is famous for its *Tafelspitz*. This is a recipe for venison which stipulates a 1986 Austrian Blauburgunder. This might be hard to find outside Austria. I suggest a Pinot Noir be used instead.

2 tbsp oil
1 oz/25 g butter
8 medallions of venison
2 shallots, peeled and finely chopped
bouquet garni
4 oz/100 g mushrooms, sliced
1 wineglass of red wine (see above)
¼ pt/150 ml reduced game stock
salt and cayenne pepper
1 oz/25 g chilled butter in pieces

Heat the oil and butter in a pan and fry the medallions on both sides to brown and seal, ensuring that the medallions stay rare. Keep warm in a low oven.

For the sauce, fry the shallots in the pan used to fry the venison over a gentle heat until soft. Add the bouquet garni and stir in the mushrooms. Cook for 1 minute more. Pour over wine and add stock. Reduce slightly and season with salt and cayenne. Whisk in the butter. To serve, pour a puddle of sauce onto 4 warmed plates and arrange the venison medallions on top.

◆

GRIESKNÖDEL MIT GRÜNEN PARADEISERN
(*Semolina Dumplings with Green Tomato Compôte*)

This curiosity, from the restaurant Taubenkobel in Schützen-am-Gebirge, is extremely good.

for the tomato compôte
6 oz/175 g green tomatoes, in strips
6 oz/175 g green apples, peeled, cored and finely chopped
6 oz/175 g brown sugar
juice of 3 oranges and 3 lemons

for the dumplings
2 oz/50 g butter
2 oz/50 g sugar
1 tbsp rum
grated zest of half an orange
½ pt/300 ml milk
2 oz/50 g semolina
1 egg, beaten
4 oz/100 g crushed nuts

to serve
8 oz/225 g fresh blackberries
¼ pt/150 ml soured cream

For the tomato compôte, place all the ingredients in a bowl and mix well. Leave to marinate overnight.

To make the dumplings, melt the butter in a pan over a low heat and add the sugar, rum and orange zest. Add the milk and bring to the boil. Stir in the semolina and simmer for 2 minutes. Take off the heat then beat in the egg. Leave to cool for 2 hours.

Shape the mixture into dumplings 1 in/2.5 cm across and poach in simmering water. Roll in crushed nuts.

Transfer the compôte to a pan and slowly bring to the boil. Simmer for 10 minutes.

To serve, spoon a little compôte onto a plate then add a few blackberries and soured cream. Place the dumplings on top.

WEINMOUSSE
(*Wine Mousse*)

The chef at König von Ungarn recommends Georg Stiegelmar's 1987 Bouvier Beerenauslese for this dish. If you do not happen to have this in your cellar, any Austrian *Beerenauslese* will do.

½ pt/300 ml sweet white wine
a few drops vanilla essence
3 oz/75 g sifted icing sugar
1 sachet gelatine
1 egg yolk
½ pt/300 ml double cream

Place the wine, vanilla essence and icing sugar in a pan and bring to the boil. Remove from the heat. Transfer 4 tbsp of the liquid to a small bowl and sprinkle in the gelatine to dissolve. Return to the pan and stir in. Cool and chill until on the point of setting. Whisk the egg yolk and cream until soft peaks are formed. Fold this carefully into the wine mixture. Pour into a pretty serving dish and leave to set in the fridge.

APFEL-NUSSKUCHEN MIT WEINSCHAUMEIS UND TREBERNSABAYONE
(*Apple Cake with Ice-cream and Grappa Sabayon*)

Zur Rossmühle is a famous old restaurant in the town of Tulln on the Danube. This recipe calls for *Eiswein*, which might seem an extravagance outside Austria. In Austria itself, *Eiswein* is relatively easy to come by.

for the ice-cream
½ pt/300 ml *Eiswein*
4 oz/100 g unsalted butter
4 egg yolks

for the cake
1 lb/450 g dessert apples
white wine for poaching
sugar to taste

piece of cinnamon
4 cloves
3 oz/75 g unsalted butter
4 oz/100 g sugar
4 eggs, separated
3 oz/75 g biscuit crumbs
3 oz/75 g crushed nuts
1 level tsp baking powder

for the sabayon
2 egg yolks
2 oz/50 g sugar
2 tbsp Grappa

Make the ice-cream first. Heat the wine in a pan. Add butter and stir to melt. Pour into the beaten egg yolks, whisking until the mixture cools. Pour into a freezer container and freeze until almost frozen. Remove and beat. Return to freeze completely; or use an ice-cream maker.

Peel, core and quarter the apples. Poach them in the wine with sugar and spices until tender but still firm. Remove the spices. Beat the butter with half the sugar until it is light and fluffy.

Add the egg yolks and crumbs alternately, little by little. Stir in the nuts and baking powder. Add the remaining sugar.

Beat the egg whites stiff and fold gently into the mixture.

Lay the apples in a buttered and sugared oven-proof dish. Smooth over the nut mixture. Cook in a bain-marie in a pre-heated oven Gas 4 350°F (180°C) for 40 minutes or until the top is firm to the touch.

For the sabayon, beat the yolks, sugar and Grappa over a low heat until the mixture is slightly thickened and frothy. Pour into a cold bowl and cool over ice.

Serve the apple cake with a scoop of ice-cream and sabayon.

With thanks to Jill Cox for her invaluable help in the preparation of these recipes.

---◆---

APPENDIX

◆

THE AUSTRIAN WINE LAW OF 1985

In the light of the 1985 wine scandal, the Austrian Ministry of Agriculture and Forestry imposed stringent laws to combat fraud and other wine malpractices. Amendments have been added to these laws, most notably provision for *Strohwein*, which were not included in the original measures; more recently (1991), the law has been altered to stipulate maximum permitted yields: these are 60 hl/ha for white wines and 75 hl/ha for reds. (These might be altered again in 1992.) These still seem a little high and quality wine producers already produce far less, but it should be borne in mind that, with the PLC (*plafond limité de classement*), most French AOC yields are at a similar level.

The 1985 law was obviously an attempt to tighten up existing legislation in order to prevent further blows to the country's export business. The *Prädikat* remained based on the German system. This of course was intended to please the country that is still Austria's major customer for wine; hence the inclusion of *Beerenauslese* and *Trockenbeerenauslese* and other terms traditionally alien to Austria.

◆

QUALITY CATEGORIES

Tafelwein Minimum 13° KMW (ie sugar content) (63° *Oechsle*) in must weight; with the exception of *Bergweine* (wines from slopes over 26 percent), it may not be bottled in 75 cl or 70 cl bottles.

Landwein *Tafelwein* from one specific region; minimum 11.5° alcohol and 6 g/l residual sugar; minimum must weight: 14° KMW.

Qualitätswein From a single wine region; from authorised grape varieties; must be typical of the grape variety; must be officially tested and display a test number; minimum of 9° alcohol for whites and 8.5° for reds; may be chaptalised by up to 4.5 kilos of sugar per 100 litres, maximum 19° KMW for whites and 20° KMW for reds; minimum 15° KMW (73° *Oechsle*) in must weight.

Kabinett Must qualify as a *Qualitätswein*; must have a minimum must weight of 17° KMW (84° *Oechsle*); may not be chaptalised; maximum alcohol content 12.7°; maximum residual sugar 9 g/l.

Prädikatswein May not be chaptalised; must come from one region only; residual sugar level must be achieved naturally; no *Süssreserve* (sweet concentrated grape juice) may be added, nor may the fermentation be stopped by artificial means; must have benefited from an official examination; must be officially tested, have a test number and carry a vintage date. The grades are:

–**Spätlese** Minimum 19° KMW (94° *Oechsle*); only fully ripened grapes may be used.

–**Auslese** Minimum 21° KMW (105° *Oechsle*); all underripe or faulty grapes must be extracted.

–**Eiswein** Minimum 25° KMW (127° *Oechsle*); the grapes must be harvested and pressed while frozen.

–**Beerenauslese** Minimum of 25° KMW (127° *Oechsle*); must be made from overripe or nobly rotten grapes.

–**Ausbruch** Minimum 27° KMW (138° *Oechsle*); must be made from overripe, nobly rotten, or naturally shrivelled grapes.

–**Trockenbeerenauslese** At least 30° KMW (156° *Oechsle*); must be made from nobly rotten, overripe or shrivelled berries.

◆

HOW TO READ AN AUSTRIAN WINE LABEL

Looking at a bottle of Austrian wine, the drinker may deduce everything that he or she needs to know about the grape varieties, origins, vintage date, quality level, producer, alcohol content and amount down to unfermented sugar in the wine.

– Starting at the top, the red, white and red (Austria's national colours) banderol gives the official identity of the wine. From the figures written here, the origin of the contents can be determined.

– At the top of the label the words *Wein aus Österreich*, or *Österreichischer Wein* indicate that the wine is made from 100 percent Austrian grapes. More specific designations may only be used when the grapes come entirely from a delimited region such as Kamptal-Donauland or the Wachau. When it comes to *Qualitätsweine*, all *Kabinett* and *Prädikat* wines must display their region of origin.

– Next come the grape variety and vintage date, indicating that at least 85 percent of the wine comes from this cultivar and vintage.

– The quality levels (see below) are then stated, these may be *Tafelwein* (table wine), *Landwein* (country wine), *Qualitätswein*, *Spätlese*, *Auslese*, *Eiswein*, *Strohwein*, *Beerenauslese*, *Ausbruch* or, *Trockenbeerenauslese*.

– The *Staatliche Prüfnummer* certifies that the wine has been examined by a state commission.

– Next, the producer or bottler is shown on every label.

– Alcohol content is given in percentage with a maximum discrepancy of 1.5 percent.

– Finally, unfermented residual sugar is stated in g/l: dry, or *trocken*, wines may have up to 4 g/l; half-dry, or *halbtrocken*, up to 9 g/l; half-sweet, or *halbsüss*, up to 18 g/l; sweet, or *süss* wines, are those over 18 g/l.

◆

RECENT VINTAGES

1990 The summer saw the same drought that affected large tracts of Europe during 1990. The estates where the vines are irrigated (for example in the Wachau) did not suffer. Good winemakers made superlative wines.

1989 A reasonable crop, but disappointing. Variable quality; the better wines came from Burgenland and Styria where growers were able to pick late. Musty wines from the Thermenregion.

1988 A huge crop of more than 3.5 million hectolitres. Good spring and summer weather; rain in September. Earlier-picked grapes sometimes made dilute wines.

1987 An abominable year saved by good autumn weather. Good wines, though occasionally sharp.

1986 A very good year, some winemakers described it as "the vintage of the century". Good extract and acidity.

1985 Very small harvest. Spring frosts destroyed 95 percent of vines in the Weinviertel and caused widespread damage elsewhere. However, some very good wines, including reds from the Burgenland and long-lived Sauvignon Blancs from Styria.

1984 A poor year; the better wines came from Styria and the Weinviertel.

1983 Although at first hailed as the greatest post-war vintage, later criticised for poor acidity.

1982 The biggest crop on record: nearly five million hectolitres. Some good wines.

1981 Notable only for late-picked sweet wines.

1980 Not a good year throughout most of Austria.

1979 A perfect flowering, hot summer and sunny autumn produced excellent quality wines.

1978 A cold, dry year. Generally mediocre wines.

1977 Excellent weather throughout the growing season. Especially good Rieslings and Grüner Veltliners from Lower Austria.

1976 Changeable weather which improved in late autumn. Poor quality, though better for *Trockenbeerenauslese* and *Ausbruch* from Burgenland.

1975 Average quality.

1974 Very poor.

1973 A very good year, particularly for the Rieslings and Grüner Veltliners from Lower Austria.

1972 Very poor.

1971 Excellent year, long-lasting wines.

1970 Poor.

WINE PRODUCERS MENTIONED IN THIS BOOK

Aigner, Wolfgang
Weinzierl 53, 3500 Krems
Tel (02732) 84558
Alphart, Karl
Wiener Strasse 46
2514 Traiskirchen
Tel (02252) 52328
Alzinger, Leo
3601 Unterloiben 11
Tel (02732) 59125
Artner, Hans
2465 Höflein 58
Tel (02162) 3142
Barmherzigen Brüder
Esterházystrasse 26
7000 Eisenstadt
Tel (02682) 601/499
**Kelleramt Benediktinerstift
Gottweig**
Weinbaubetriebe
Dr Wolfgang Unger
Kirchengasse 19
2511 Furth bei Göttweig
Tel (02732) 85895
Bernreiter, Gertrude
Amtsstrasse 24–26, 1210 Wien
Tel (0222) 393680
Bichler (*see* **Leberl**)
Biegler, Manfred
Wiener Strasse 16–18
2352 Gumpoldskirchen
Tel (02252) 62196
Breyer, Leopold
Amtsstrasse 15
1210 Wien-Jedlersdorf
Tel (0222) 394148
Bründlmayer, Wilhelm
Zwettler Strasse 23
3550 Langenlois
Tel (02734) 2172
Chorherren Klosterneuburg
Stiftsweingut, Am Renninger 2
3400 Klosterneuburg
Tel (02243) 6375
**Dinstlgut Loiben
(Winzergenossenschaft)**
3601 Unterloiben 51
Tel (02732) 85516
Ditz, Karl
Weingut Lehenhof
Weinzierl 17, 3500 Krems
Tel (02732) 83390
Dolle, Peter
3491 Strass im Strassertale 2

Tel (02735) 2326
Elfenhof, Holler
Baumgartengasse 11
7071 Rust am See
Tel (02685) 470
Feiler-Artinger
Hauptstrasse 3
7071 Rust am See
Tel (02685) 237
Feuerwehr-Wagner
Grinzinger Strasse 53
1190 Wien-Heiligenstadt
Tel (0222) 322442
Fischer, Christian
Hauptstrasse 33, 2500 Soos
Tel (02252) 87130
Freie Weingärtner Wachau
3601 Dürnstein 107
Tel (02711) 371/217/218
Fritsch, Karl
Oberstockstall 24
3470 Kirchberg am Wagram
Tel (02279) 27403
**Gesellmann, Englebert and
Maria**
Langegasse 65
7301 Deutschkreutz
Tel (02613) 360
Geyerhof, Familie Maier
Oberfucha 3
3511 Furth bei Gottweig
Tel (02739) 2259
Geymüller, Domäne Baron
Schloss Hollenburg 57
3506 Krems
Tel (02739) 2229
Gisperg, Johann
Hauptstrasse 14
2524 Teesdorf
Tel (02253) 81464
Glatzer, Walter
2464 Gottlesbrunn 76
Tel (02162) 8486
Grabner-Schierer
Hauptstrasse 55, 2500 Sooss
Tel (02252) 87392
Grinschgl, Max
Gundersdorf 50
8511 St Stefan ob Stainz
Tel (03463) 813012
Gross, Alois
8461 Ratsch 10
Tel (03453) 2527
Haimer, Emmerich and Hertha

Brunngasse 42, 2170 Poysdorf
Tel (02552) 2642
Heinrich, Erich
Wassergasse 2, 7122 Gols
Tel (02173) 2302
Hiedler, Dr Bruno
Holzplaz 2
3550 Langenlois
Tel (02734) 2468
Hirschmugl, Franz
Demmerkogel-Sausal
8444 St Andrä-Höch
Tel (03456) 2684
Hirtzberger, Franz
Kremser Strasse 8
3620 Spitz an der Donau
Tel (02713) 2209
Hofer, Friedrich
Badener Strasse 25
2352 Gumpoldskirchen
Tel (02252) 62282
Holler (*see* **Elfenhof**)
Iby, Anton and Johanna
Kirchengasse 4a
7312 Horitschon
Tel (02610) 2292
Igler, Hans
Langegasse 49
7301 Deutschkreutz
Tel (02613) 365
Jamek, Josef
3610 Joching
Tel (02715) 2235
Jurtschitsch
Sonnhof
Rudolfstrasse 39
3550 Langenlois
Tel (02734) 2116
Kappel, Günter
Steinriegel 25
8442 Kitzeck
Tel (03456) 2347
Kattus, Johann
Am Hof 8
1011 Wien
Tel (0222) 364350
Kerschbaum, Paul
Hauptstrasse 37
7312 Horitschon
Tel (02610) 2392
Kierlinger, Martin
Kahlenberger Strasse 20
1190 Wien-Nussdorf
Tel (0222) 372264

Knoll, Emmerich
3601 Unterloiben 10
Tel (02732) 69355
Kölbl, Ernst
3743 Röschitz 124
Tel (02984) 2779
Kollwentz, Anton
Hauptstrasse 120
7051 Grosshöflein
Tel (02682) 5158
Koller, Johann
Feldbaum 35, 8524 Bad Gams
Tel (03462) 2923
Kopfensteiner, Manfred
7474 Deutsch Schützen 38
Tel (03365) 2236
Körper-Faulhammer
Schützenhof, Berg 159
7474 Deutsch Schützen
Tel (03365) 2203
Kracher, Alois
Weinlaubenhof
Apetloner Strasse 27
7142 Illmitz
Tel (02175) 24202
Krutzler, Hermann
7474 Deutsch Schützen 84
Tel (03365) 2242
Kurz, Franz and Antonia
Neustiftgasse 13
2352 Gumpoldskirchen
Tel (02252) 62414
Lackner-Tinnacher
Steinbach 12, 8462 Gamlitz
Tel (03453) 2142
Lagler, Karl
Rote-Tor-Gasse 10
3620 Spitz an der Donau
Tel (02713) 2516
Landauer, Bruno and Martha
Hadyngasse 5
7071 Rust am See
Tel (02685) 278
Lazarus, Josef
Langegg 20
8511 St Stefan ob Stainz
Tel (03463) 81405
Leberl, Josef
Hauptstrasse 91, 7051 Grosshöflein
Tel (02682) 34853
Leberwurst, Josef
Obere Landstrasse 27
2191 Höbersbrunn
Tel (02574) 2251
Lehrner, Paul
Hauptstrasse 56

7312 Horitschon
Tel (02610) 2403
Leth, Franz
Kirchengasse 6
3481 Fels am Wagram
Tel (02738) 2240
Lust, Josef
Hauptstrasse 39, 2054 Haugsdorf
Tel (02944) 2287
Mad, Wilhelm (*see* **Marienberg**)
Marienberg (Haus),
Wilhelm Mad
Antonigasse 1, 7063 Oggau
Tel (02685) 7207
Malat-Bründlmayer, Gerald
Lindengasse 27, 3511 Furth-Palt
Tel (02732) 2934
Malteser, Ritterorden (*see*
Moser, Lenz)
2024 Mailberg
Tel (02732) 85541
Mantlerhof
Hauptstrasse 50
3494 Brunn im Felde
Tel (02735) 8248
Mayer am Pfarrplatz
Pfarrplatz 2
1190 Wien-Heiligenstadt
Tel (0222) 373361
Messermayer, Johann
2464 Göttlesbrunn 154
Tel (02162) 8472
Metternich'sche Weingüter
Dominikanerplatz 11
3500 Krems-Strass
Tel (02735) 2213
Minkowitsch, Roland
2261 Angern
Mannersdorf an der March 64
Tel (02283) 2583/2308
Moser, Lenz
Lenz Moser Strasse 4–6
3495 Rohrendorf bei Krems
Tel (02732) 85541
Müller, Günter
Gussendorf 5
8522 Gross St Florian
Tel (03464) 2234
Neumayer, Ludwig
3130 Inzersdorf 22
Tel (02782) 2985
Neumeister, Albert
8345 Straden 42
Tel (03473) 308
Neustifter, Reinhard
2162 Falkenstein 143

Tel (02554) 7723
Nigl, Josef
Priel 8, 3541 Senftenberg
Tel (02719) 2609
Nikolaihof, (Nikolaus Saahs)
3512 Mautern, Wachau
Tel (02732) 82901
Nittnaus, Hans
Untere Hauptstrasse 49
7122 Gols
Tel (02173) 2248
Opitz, Willi
Quergasse 11, 7142 Illmitz
Tel (02175) 2084
Osberger, Helmut
3491 Strass bei Krems
Tel (02735) 7272
Pasler-Bäck
Untere Hauptstrasse 53
7093 Jois
Tel (02160) 7203
Pfaffl, Roman
Hauptstrasse 24, 2100 Stetten
Tel (02262) 46323
Pichler, Franz Xaver
3601 Oberloiben 27
Tel (02732) 85375
Pitnauer, Hans
2464 Gottlesbrunn 9–10
Tel (02162) 8249
Platzer, Manfred
Göttlesbrunn, Pichla 25
8355 Tieschen
Tel (03475) 2331
Pleil, Josef
Aldergasse 32, 2120 Wolkersdorf
Tel (02245) 2407
Polz, Reinhold and Söhne
Grassnitzberg 54
8471 Spielfeld
Tel (03453) 2301
Prager, Franz
3610 Weissenkirchen 48
Tel (02715) 2248
Prieler, Engelbert
Hauptstrasse 181
7081 Schützen am Gebirge
Tel (02684) 2229
Reinisch, Johann
Johanneshof
Am Raiffeisenplatz 6
2523 Tattendorf
Tel (02253) 81423
Salomon, Heinrich
2162 Falkenstein 24
Tel (02554) 7703

Salomon, Erich
Undhof, Undstrasse 10
3504 Krems-Stein
Tel (02732) 83226
Sattler, Willi
Sernau 2, 8462 Gamlitz
Tel (03453) 2556
Schafler, Andreas
Wiener Strasse 9/11
2514 Traiskirchen
Tel (02252) 52378
Schandl, Peter
Haydngasse 3, 7071 Rust am See
Tel (02685) 265
Schellmann, Gottfried
Wiener Strasse 41
2352 Gumpoldskirchen
Tel (02252) 62218
Schierer (see **Grabner-Schierer**)
Schilling, Herbert
Langenzersdorfer Strasse 54
1210 Wien Strebersdorf
Tel (0222) 394189
Schindler, Franz
Neustiftgasse 6
7072 Mörbisch am See
Tel (02685) 8326
Schlumberger
Gürtler AG
Scheringgasse 4, 1140 Wien
Tel (0222) 971634
Schmidl, Franz
3601 Dürnstein 21
Tel (02711) 224
Schröck, Heidi
Rathauplatz 8, 7071 Rust am See
Tel (02685) 229/444
Schuster, Rosi
Hauptstrasse 59, 7011 Zagersdorf
Tel (02687) 8111
Seyffertitz, Cari (see **Stürgkh**)
Silberbichlerhof (Hutter)
Fritz Hutter
3512 Mautern, Wachau
Tel (02732) 83004
Sonnhof (see **Jurtschitsch**)
Stadlmann, Johann
Wiener Strasse 41

2514 Traiskirchen
Tel (02252) 52343
Stiegelmar, Georg
Untere Hauptstrasse 60
7122 Gols
Tel (02173) 2203
Stift Klosterneuburg
Am Renninger 2
3400 Klosterneuburg
Tel (02243) 6375
Strell, Josef
3710 Radlbrunn 138
Tel (02956) 2466
Stürgkh
Graflich Stürgkh'sches Weingut
8493 Klöch 29
Tel (03475) 2223
Szemes, Tibor
Weinhoferplatz 7, 7423 Pinkafeld
Tel (03357) 2367
Taubenschuss, Helmut
Körnergasse 2, 2170 Poysdorf
Tel (02552) 2589
Tement, Manfred
Zieregg 13, 8461 Berghausen
Tel (03453) 4101
Topf, Johann
Herrengasse 6
3491 Strass im Strassertale
Tel (02735) 491
Triebaumer, Ernst
Raiffeisenstrasse 9
7071 Rust am See
Tel (02685) 528
Triebaumer, Paul
Neue Gasse 18
7071 Rust am See
Tel (02685) 6135
Umathum, Josef
St Andräer Strasse 7
7132 Frauenkirchen
Tel (02171) 2173
Wachter
Arkadenhof
7474 Deutsch Schützen 26
Tel (03365) 2245
Wallner, Anna and Josef
7474 Deutsch Schützen 117

Tel (03365) 2295
WBS Retz (Weinbauschule)
Landwirtschaftliche
Fachschule in Retz
Seeweg 2, 2070 Retz
Tel (02942) 2202
Weinrieder, Barbara
Untere Ortsstrasse 44
2170 Kleinhadersdorf bei Poysdorf
Tel (02552) 2241
Weinkellerei Burgenland
Am Rusterberg
7071 Rust am See
Tel (02685) 544
Weiss, Josef
Wiener Strasse 27
2352 Gumpoldskirchen
Tel (02252) 62539
Weninger, Franz
Florianigasse 11, 7312 Horitschon
Tel (02610) 2531
Wenzel, Robert
Hauptstrasse 29, 7071 Rust am See
Tel (02685) 287
Wieder, Juliane
Lange Zeile 76
7311 Neckenmarkt
Tel (02610) 2438
Wieder, Stefan
Lange Zeile 17, 7311 Neckenmarkt
Tel (02610) 2474
Wieninger, Barbara
Stammersdorfer Strasse 78
1210 Wien-Stammersdorf
Tel (0222) 394106
Wiesler, Gisela
7474 Deutsch Schützen 91
Tel (03365) 21194
Winkler-Hermaden
Schloss Kapfenstein
8353 Kapfenstein 105
Tel (03157)2322
Winzer Krems
Sandgrube 13, 3500 Krems/Donau
Tel (02732) 85511
Zull, Werner
2073 Schrattenthal 9
Tel (02946) 292

◆

RECOMMENDED RESTAURANTS

VIENNA
Altwienerhof Herklotzgasse 6, 1150 Vienna.
Tel 837145 Modern; luxurious.

Eckel Sieveringstrasse 46, Sievering. Tel 323218
Smart restaurant not far from Grinzing which
provides an alternative to eating in a *Heurige*.

Good wine list. Chancellor Vranitzky is occasionally seen here.

Korso Mahlerstrasse 2, 1010 Vienna. Tel 51516/546 One of Vienna's top restaurants; combines modern and Austrian traditional cuisine.

Schnattl Lange Gasse 40, 1080 Vienna. Tel 423400 Good kitchen, rustic interior.

Steirereck Rasumofskygasse 2, 1030 Vienna. Tel 7133168 One of Vienna's best restaurants.

Steinerne Eule Halbgasse 30, 1070 Vienna. Tel 932250 Rather modern style.

Zu den Drei Husaren Weihburggasse 4, 1010 Vienna. Tel 5121092 Traditional Viennese restaurant; luxurious.

Zum Herkner Strasse 123, 1170 Dornbacher. Tel 4610554 An old *Edelbeisl* (up-market bistro) specialising in hearty Viennese food. Interesting wines. Another favourite of Chancellor Vranitzky.

WACHAU

Die Tränke Dürnstein. Tel (02711) 230 Useful wine bar in the centre of historic Dürnstein with a selection of good Wachau wines.

Florianihof (Weissenkirchen), Wösendorf. Tel (02715) 2212 Decent if unexciting restaurant in the heart of the Wachau.

Jamek Joching. Tel (02715) 2235 Josef Jamek's own restaurant, and his wines.

Landhaus Bacher Mautern. Tel (02732) 82937 One of Lower Austria's very top restaurants. In summer try to sit in the garden to avoid the piped music. Excellent wine-list.

Loibnerhof Unterloiben. Tel (02732) 82890 Good food in slightly drab surroundings. The attraction here is the wines of Emmerich Knoll.

Schloss Dürnstein Dürnstein. Tel (02711) 212 Lovely old *Schloss* with stunning views of the Wachau from its tastefully decorated rooms. The kitchen is not so noteworthy.

KAMPTAL-DONAULAND

Am Förthof Krems-Stein. Tel (02732) 3345 Restaurant and hotel at the gates of the Wachau. Decent food and wines, bizarre service.

Schickh Klein-Wien, Göttweig. Tel (02736) 218 Good food in a rather uncomfortable restaurant beside the railway line. The monastery is perched above the valley. Good local wines.

DONAULAND-CARNUNTUM

Gasthaus zur Traube Feuersbrunn. Tel (02738) 2298 Refined modern cooking by Toni Mörwald disciple of Gerer at Vienna's Korso restaurant.

Gut Oberstockstall Kirchberg bei Wagram. Tel (02279) 2335 Simple but well thought out food in the renaissance *Schloss*.

Zum Roten Wolf Bhanstrafe 58, Langenlebarn. Tel (02272) 2567 This is one of Austria's best restaurants, though in an impossible location beside the railway line. Very good modern cooking and good wines.

Zur Rossmühle Hauptplatz 12–13, Tulln. Tel (02272) 2411 A smart restaurant with many local specialities and a good wine list.

WEINVIERTEL

Stadthotel Eggenburg Kremser Strasse 8, 3730 Eggenburg. Tel (02984) 3532 Traditional.

Weinlandhof Kleinhadersdorf, Bundesstrasse 67, 2170 Poysdorf. Tel (02552) 2625 Extremely rustic-style hotel-restaurant.

Weinschlössl 2070 Retz. Tel (02942) 3224 Very rustic style.

THERMENREGION

Jagdhof Guntramsdorf. Tel (02236) 52225 Stylish restaurant not far from Gumpoldskirchen. Good wines.

Jahreszeiten Hochstrasse 17, 2830 Perchtoldsdorf. Tel (0222) 865329 Exceptionally good restaurant and wine list to match. Convenient for Vienna.

Primavera Weilburg Strasse 3, Baden. Tel (02252) 85551 Small, bistro-style restaurant with good, modern cooking and decent wines.

NEUSIEDLERSEE-HÜGELLAND

Am Spitz Purbach. Tel (02683) 219/5519 Purbach has no Turkish restaurants. This hotel-restaurant also acts as a showpiece for the Schwarz family's vineyards.

Reisinger Haupt Strasse 83, Pöttsching. Tel (02631) 2212 Very good restaurant specialising in local wine and produce.

Reisner Haupt Strasse 141, Forchtenstein. Tel (02626) 63139 Rather more rustic food here but a good wine list for all that.

Rusterhof Rathausplatz 18, Rust. Tel (02685)
6416 In the old town: limited wine list.
Taubenkobel Haupt Strasse 33, Schützen am
Gebirge. Tel (02684) 2297 The best restaurant in
Burgenland. The food is modern and inventive
and the owners charming. Exemplary wine list.

NEUSIEDLERSEE
Barth-Stuben Franz-Liszt-Gasse 37, 7100
Neusiedl am See. Tel (02167) 2625

CENTRAL BURGENLAND
Gasthaus Zur Traube 7311 Neckenmarkt.
Tel (02619) 2256 Rustic.

SOUTH BURGENLAND
Raffel Hauptplatz 6, 8380 Jennersdorf.
Tel (03154) 6622 Good, simple cooking.
Schwabenhof (Hotel) Hagensdorf 22, 7522
Heiligenbrunn. Tel (03324) 333 Reports of good
local specialities.

SOUTHEAST STYRIA
Buschenschank Albert Neumeister 8345
Straden. Tel (03473) 308 Specialities: home-
made sausage, tongue.
Schlosswirt Schloss Kapfenstein, 8353
Kapfenstein. Tel (03157) 2202 The family also
own the winery Schloss Kapfenstein.

WEST STYRIA
Jagawirt Greisdorf. Tel (03143) 8105
A restaurant in *Schilcher* country with a good list
of local wines and good food to accompany them.

SOUTH STYRIA
Sattlerhof Gamlitz. Tel (03453) 4454 The place
to sample some of the wines of this top producer;
simple if excellent food to match.
Weinhof Kappel Kitzeck. Tel (03456) 2347
Restaurant, hotel and winery on one of the
highest cultivated hills in Styria. Stocks wines
besides the estate's own and the food is fine.

◆

BIBLIOGRAPHY

Breitschneider, Dr A *Denkschrift zur 70
jährigen Bestandesfeier der Höheren Bundes-
Lehranstalt und Bundesversuchstation für Wein,
Obst und Gartenbau in Klosterneuburg* (1930)
 von Conrad, P L *Beschreibung des Ruster
Weinbaues in Ahrenlese des Georgikons Ersten
Bandes, Erstes heft* (1819)
 Deutsch, G 'Die Geschichte des Weinbaues
und Weinhandels in Österreich und Ungarn nach
den Quellen dargestellt' *Österreichisch-Ungarische
Revue* Vol 13
 Endriss, G *Vom Weinbau im Burgenland
(Österreich) und besonders in Rust am
Neusiedlersee* (1973)
 Goethe H *Handbuch der Ampelographie* (1887)
 Schlumberger Edler von Goldeck, R
*Weinhandel und Weinbau im Kaiserstaate
Österreich 1804–1918* (1937)
 Ritter von Heintl, F *Die Landwirtschaft des
österreichischen Kaiserthumes* (1835)
 Hyams, E *Dionysius, A Social History of the
Wine Vine* (1965)
 Kern, A *Gumpoldskirchens Weinbau einst und

jetzt. Eine Culture-Skizze* (1985)
 Lantschbauer, R and Barwisch, S *Das Buch
vom Steierischen Wein* (1987)
 Lantschbauer, R and Barwisch, S *Weinland
Österreich* (1989)
 Leskoschek, Dr F *Geschichte des Weinbaues in
der Steiermark* (1934)
 Lobnig R and Oswald, C *Der Schilcher* (1985)
 Maier-Bruck, F *Das Grosse Sacher Kochbuch*
(Vienna 1975)
 Gault Millau *Österreich: Guide für Gourmets
1991* (1990)
 Reinhartz M and Wagner, C *Österreichs
Ländliche Küche* (1990)
 Schams, F *Vollständige Beschreibung
sämmtlicher berühmter Weingebirge in Österreich,
Mähren und Böhmen in statistisch, topographisch-
naturhistorischer und ökonomischer Hinsicht* (1835)
 Steurer, R *Österreichischer Weinführer* 2 vols
(1990)
 Steurer, R *Wiener Heurigenführer: Die
Original-Buschenschenken* (1989)
 Traxler, H *Das Österreichische Weinbuch* (1962)